RAVENS:
SPASSKY VS. FISCHER

Tom Morton-Smith

RAVENS: SPASSKY VS. FISCHER

OBERON BOOKS
LONDON

WWW.OBERONBOOKS.COM

First published in 2019 by Oberon Books Ltd
521 Caledonian Road, London N7 9RH
Tel: +44 (0) 20 7607 3637 / Fax: +44 (0) 20 7607 3629
e-mail: info@oberonbooks.com
www.oberonbooks.com

PB ISBN: 9781786829320
E ISBN: 9781786829337

Cover: Image by SWD / Photography by Shaun Webb

eBook conversion in India.

10 9 8 7 6 5 4 3 2 1

For Hester

With thanks to Jack Bradley, Rose Cobbe,
Annabelle Comyn and Jen Tan

Ravens: Spassky vs. Fischer was first performed in a Hampstead Theatre World Premiere on 29 November 2019 with the following cast:

GUÐMUNDUR ÞÓRARINSSON	Gunnar Cauthery
MAX EUWE	Simon Chandler
FRED CRAMER /	
LINA GRUMETTE	Buffy Davis
LOTHAR SCHMID	Philip Desmeules
BOBBY FISCHER	Robert Emms
WILLIAM LOMBARDY /	
HENRY KISSINGER	Solomon Israel
IIVO NEI	Beruce Khan
REGINA FISCHER	Emma Pallant
BORIS SPASSKY	Ronan Raftery
NIKOLAI KROGIUS	Rebecca Scroggs
EFIM GELLER	Gyuri Sarossy
SÆMUNDUR 'SÆMI-ROKK' PÁLSSON	Gary Shelford

Creative Team

Writer	Tom Morton-Smith
Director	Annabelle Comyn
Designer	Jamie Vartan
Lighting	Howard Harrison
Composer & Sound	Philip Stewart
Video	Jack Phelan
Movement	Mike Ashcroft
Casting	Juliet Horsley CDG

Characters

The Americans
BOBBY FISCHER – *challenger*
FRED CRAMER – *manager*
HENRY KISSINGER – *foreign policy advisor*
LINA GRUMETTE – *chess mother*
WILLIAM LOMBARDY – *Fischer's second*
REGINA FISCHER – *communist*

The Soviets
BORIS SPASSKY – *world champion*
NIKOLAI KROGIUS – *psychologist*
EFIM GELLER – *strategist*
IIVO NEI – *sparring partner*

Others
GUÐMUNDUR ÞÓRARINSSON – *organiser*
MAX EUWE – *President of FIDE*
LOTHAR SCHMID – *arbiter*
SÆMUNDUR 'SÆMI-ROKK' PÁLSSON – *policeman*

Author's Notes

The play takes place in July and August 1972.

Included are the move lists for the twenty-one chess games of the championship – though it is not expected that each game be faithfully recreated. The games need not take the form of a literal chess game. The form of the contest matters less than the result.

Lines within [square brackets] are to be spoken in Russian. Translations can be found at the end of the script.

Russian characters, when speaking 'Russian' amongst themselves, speak with the actors' own accents. When the Russian characters speak English with the English-speaking characters they should do so with 'Russian' accents. All other characters should be assumed to be speaking English with accents consistent with their nationalities.

Act One

1.

The Loftleiðir Hotel, Reykjavík.

EFIM GELLER, NIKOLAI KROGIUS and IIVO NEI are waiting.

EFIM: [Stop.]

IIVO: [What?]

EFIM: [Stop shaking your leg.]

IIVO: [I'm not shaking my …]

EFIM: [You are.]

IIVO: [I can shake my leg if I want.]

EFIM: [Why does a man shake his leg, Nikolai? Is it symptomatic of something?]

NIKOLAI: [A soothing ritual. Don't read too much into it.]

EFIM: Are you anxious, Iivo?

IIVO: Don't we have reason to be?

EFIM: It's a weakness of character.

NIKOLAI: That goes a bit far.

EFIM: It's what the American will think.

NIKOLAI: Is the coffee good?

EFIM: Yes.

GUÐMUNDUR ÞÓRARINSSON enters.

GUÐMUNDUR: Is Mr Spassky … Comrade Spassky …? I thought he was …?

NIKOLAI: He's in the bathroom.

GUÐMUNDUR: Ah. We're still waiting on Mr Euwe and Mr Schmid …

IIVO: And Mr Fischer.

GUÐMUNDUR: Yes. Very good.

EFIM: Any word from …?

GUÐMUNDUR: I think we should probably wait for …

NIKOLAI: Of course.

Silence.

GUÐMUNDUR: I'll just go and see if … *(Exits.)*

IIVO: I'll take a cigarette.

NIKOLAI: *(Passes him a cigarette.)*

EFIM: What do you think?

IIVO: Of what?

EFIM: The Western brands.

IIVO: *(Shrugs.)* What else am I to smoke?

NIKOLAI: They're better on the lungs.

EFIM: I'll stick with what I know.

NIKOLAI: These are smoother.

EFIM: I like to feel what I'm smoking.

IIVO: I prefer the taste.

NIKOLAI: They'll give us the game.

EFIM: I'm not so sure.

NIKOLAI: They don't have a choice.

EFIM: They're scared of the Americans.

IIVO: The Chess Federation?

EFIM: The Icelanders.

NIKOLAI: They're scared it might all fall apart.

EFIM: We should have insisted on a neutral location.

IIVO: Reykjavík is neutral.

EFIM: There's an American military base not thirty miles from here.

IIVO: There's no special love between Iceland and the US.

EFIM: They are allies.

NIKOLAI: And we are trade partners – Iceland has a foot in both camps. Leave the shadows alone, Efim ... not everything is a conspiracy.

BORIS SPASSKY enters.

IIVO: We've got coffee.

BORIS: Is it good?

IIVO: Makes you feel like part of the Muscovite art set.

BORIS: When we get home ... I can get you coffee.

IIVO: Like this?

BORIS: Of course.

NIKOLAI: What Boris can get is 'coffee-flavoured drink'.

EFIM: I've asked for tea.

BORIS: Can we arrange fresh orange juice?

EFIM: I'll call reception.

BORIS: No … I meant … I would like fresh orange juice before each of the games.

NIKOLAI: Of course. Anything else?

BORIS: I don't think so.

NIKOLAI: Can I get you an orange juice now?

BORIS: Coffee's fine.

IIVO: Is Fischer sick?

EFIM: They may well say that.

IIVO: Why would he forfeit the opening game? You can't win if you don't turn up.

BORIS: I'm not worried.

IIVO: Why would he gift you an advantage?

EFIM: It's not about us, it's about the money. He is holding out for more.

IIVO: It cannot simply be the money.

NIKOLAI: He has asked for thirty percent of the door … on top of the percentage he gets for the broadcast rights.

IIVO: And the prize pot.

BORIS: Nowhere does it say that only gentlemen can play chess.

NIKOLAI: They will give us the game.

EFIM: They may not.

IIVO: They'll hardly break their own rules.

EFIM: He acts like he's already won ... he acts like a champion.

BORIS: Champions don't act like this. I don't act like this.

EFIM: Still ... they are pandering to him.

BORIS: They simply want the game to go ahead.

IIVO: How long is the flight from New York? Perhaps he is already in the air.

NIKOLAI: If he were then they would know ... if they knew then they would say.

EFIM: In any other championship ...

BORIS: In any other championship it would be Russian against Russian ... it would be Petrosian versus Smyslov ... Taimanov versus Korchnoi ... it would be you versus me.

IIVO: Taimanov is Ukrainian.

EFIM: It is the same thing ... Soviet versus Soviet ...

NIKOLAI: Petrosian is from Georgia, I believe.

IIVO: It is not the same.

BORIS: Even so ... even if it were myself versus ... I don't know ... the Danish champion ... Bent Larson ... no one would be as interested in a Dane overthrowing twenty-six years of Soviet chess dominance. Fischer is an American. It's a little bit of circus. I do not mind.

GUÐMUNDUR re-enters with MAX EUWE, LOTHAR SCHMID and FRED CRAMER.

MAX: Boris ...

BORIS: Max ...

NIKOLAI: Max …

MAX: Nikolai …

BORIS: Lothar …

LOTHAR: Boris …

IIVO: Lothar …

LOTHAR: Iivo …

MAX: Efim …

EFIM: Max …

MAX: Iivo …

FRED: Fred.

BORIS: Boris.

NIKOLAI: Nikolai.

EFIM: Efim.

IIVO: Iivo.

LOTHAR: Nikolai …

NIKOLAI: Lothar …

EFIM: Lothar …

LOTHAR: Efim …

GUÐMUNDUR: Guðmundur Þórarinsson.

BORIS: Where is Bobby Fischer?

MAX: In New York.

EFIM: This is unacceptable.

NIKOLAI: He is booked onto a plane?

MAX: No.

BORIS: How ill is he?

MAX: We have received a telegram ...

FRED: From a doctor.

MAX: ... from a doctor.

EFIM: What kind of illness?

FRED: That is a private matter.

EFIM: Does he have a cold? Is it scarlet fever? Is it the plague?

FRED: We expect him to make a full recovery.

EFIM: When?

FRED: In due time.

EFIM: Time is due! Time is past due!

NIKOLAI: Excuse me, who are you?

FRED: Fred Cramer.

NIKOLAI: And you speak for Fischer?

FRED: I do.

MAX: And he sends his apologies.

FRED: You do not need to apologise when you are ill.

BORIS: When did you receive this telegram?

FRED: Four o'clock this morning.

BORIS: May we see it?

FRED: No.

EFIM: No?

FRED: It is a private matter.

NIKOLAI: Max ... have you seen this telegram?

MAX: I ...

BORIS: Max?

MAX: No.

FRED: *(Disappointed.)*

MAX: I won't lie. I haven't seen it.

BORIS: Lothar?

LOTHAR: I haven't seen it either.

FRED: It is a piece of paper with some words. I can tell you the words. Why do you need to see it?

BORIS: Because I am trying to work out whether it is Fischer that is lying or you.

NIKOLAI: The President of the International Federation should see it. The referee ... the arbiter of the tournament ... should see it.

LOTHAR: I would like to see it.

FRED: There is no need.

NIKOLAI: Then we do not believe that it exists.

EFIM: You are covering for him.

GUÐMUNDUR: The priority above all else is the game.

NIKOLAI: Perhaps we should start making our own demands.

MAX: It would be within your rights.

NIKOLAI: It is within our rights to claim a forfeit.

MAX: That would be a shame.

GUÐMUNDUR: No one wants that.

EFIM: We might want it.

MAX: He is ill.

NIKOLAI: Then let us see the telegram.

FRED: No.

NIKOLAI: Then let us see your credentials … some official warrant … something signed by Fischer … saying that you are authorised to speak for him.

FRED: Are you serious …?

NIKOLAI: We do not know who this man is.

FRED: My name is Fred Cramer.

NIKOLAI: He claims to speak for Fischer …

FRED: I 'claim' …?!

NIKOLAI: If you do not speak for Fischer … if you are not authorised by him … if you are not in direct contact with Bobby Fischer … then you have no authority in these discussions.

EFIM: And you should leave.

NIKOLAI: Max …?

Everyone looks to MAX.

MAX: *(Capitulates.)*

FRED: *(Exits – furious.)*

MAX: We must give Fischer time. If he is ill …

EFIM: Then let him say that he is ill.

LOTHAR: We must declare that he has forfeited the first game.

GUÐMUNDUR: It is not the start that we had hoped for …

LOTHAR: … but we would still, at least, have a tournament.

IIVO: Is it better to declare the game lost, rather than forfeit?

LOTHAR: The effect would be the same.

MAX: I do not like to declare the first game lost.

LOTHAR: It would be a shame.

GUÐMUNDUR: … and not technically possible.

MAX: As President of the World Chess Federation …

GUÐMUNDUR: You can't declare a game lost before it has even begun … and if we claim the game forfeit, he may never come.

EFIM: Then Boris retains the title by default.

BORIS: It is not how I like to win.

IIVO: Fischer is the one backing down, not you.

MAX: We must postpone the game.

EFIM: No.

NIKOLAI: Absolutely not.

EFIM: There is no precedent for such a thing.

NIKOLAI: The championship has already begun. You cannot postpone the first game.

MAX: The tournament may have started … but the tournament is not the game. No pieces have been drawn

… no clock has been set ticking … there have been no opening moves …

EFIM: We attended an opening ceremony … a ceremony to mark the beginning of the contest … am I wrong?

LOTHAR: You're not wrong.

EFIM: This man gave a speech.

GUÐMUNDUR: It was my opening address.

IIVO: His opening address.

EFIM: In front of the Prime Minister of Iceland.

GUÐMUNDUR: And also the President.

EFIM: An official opening of the championship.

MAX: No clock has been started.

EFIM: Fischer is the challenger … but he refuses to challenge. Why should the Federation support him?

MAX: We will draw the pieces in two days' time.

NIKOLAI: The Soviet delegation does not agree with this postponement and the decisions taken by the Chess Federation's president.

MAX: Your objection has been noted.

EFIM: Boris?

BORIS: I want to play chess.

2

A house in Douglaston, Queens.

BOBBY FISCHER is on the phone. A VOICE on the end of the line.

VOICE: Is this Robert Fischer?

BOBBY: This is Bobby Fischer.

VOICE: This is Robert James Fischer?

BOBBY: Yes.

VOICE: Please hold for Doctor Kissinger.

    Silence. HENRY KISSINGER comes onto the line.

HENRY: Hello, Bobby?

BOBBY: *(No response.)*

HENRY: Hello? Is there …?

BOBBY: I'm here.

HENRY: Hello, Bobby.

BOBBY: Hello.

HENRY: Do you know who I am?

BOBBY: Yes.

HENRY: Do you know why I have called?

BOBBY: No.

HENRY: You don't know why I am calling?

BOBBY: I could take a guess.

HENRY: Why don't you take a guess then.

BOBBY: You think I should go to Reykjavík.

HENRY: I do think that, yes.

BOBBY: *(Silence.)*

HENRY: You are having some second thoughts ... is that fair to say, Bobby?

BOBBY: I don't know, sir.

HENRY: You don't know?

BOBBY: No, sir.

HENRY: Well, I think you are probably having some second thoughts. You have done well to get to this point. Do you not want to see it through?

BOBBY: You follow chess?

HENRY: I do.

BOBBY: Do you play?

HENRY: Enough to appreciate your skill. *(Beat.)* Do you like Communists, Bobby?

BOBBY: No, sir.

HENRY: Why don't you like Communists?

BOBBY: I don't know.

HENRY: You must have some idea.

BOBBY: I guess ...

HENRY: Yes?

BOBBY: Everything is handed to them.

HENRY: Not like you.

BOBBY: No.

HENRY: No one ever gave you anything.

BOBBY: They cheat.

HENRY: How do they cheat?

BOBBY: They work together.

HENRY: And that's cheating?

BOBBY: Yes, sir.

HENRY: And they've held the world championship since 1946.

BOBBY: Yes.

HENRY: That can't stand, can it, Bobby? Cheaters holding the world championship.

BOBBY: No.

HENRY: No. So what should we do about it, do you think? If an American player … such as yourself … were to knock them from their pedestal … that would be good, wouldn't it?

BOBBY: Yes.

HENRY: It would send out a powerful statement.

BOBBY: It would.

HENRY: What would that statement be?

BOBBY: Cheaters never prosper.

HENRY: 'Cheaters never prosper'. That's a good thing to tell the world, don't you think?

BOBBY: I was holding out for more money.

HENRY: Yes.

BOBBY: And they found more money.

HENRY: So I have heard.

BOBBY: The prize-pot has been doubled.

HENRY: But you haven't boarded that plane.

BOBBY: There are journalists outside. There are photographers. The phone has been tapped.

HENRY: I cannot speak to that. *(Beat.)* Are you scared?

BOBBY: No.

HENRY: Are you afraid?

BOBBY: No.

HENRY: What are you afraid of?

BOBBY: *(No response.)*

HENRY: They are Communists, Bobby.

BOBBY: I know that.

HENRY: To lead the world in chess is to claim a superiority of the intellect. This is a hill that they will die on. Wouldn't it be sweet to take it from them?

BOBBY: It would.

HENRY: Good. Well … I hope you will forgive me but I have other matters to attend.

BOBBY: Sure.

HENRY: The United States Government wishes you well and I wish you well.

BOBBY: Thank you, sir.

HENRY: The world is watching. You're a soldier now, Bobby.

3

Laugardalshöll arena.

BORIS, IIVO, EFIM and NIKOLAI wait backstage.

EFIM: He'll offer you his hand palm down.

BORIS: What does that mean?

EFIM: It's an American thing.

NIKOLAI: It's a dominance thing.

EFIM: If you miss the chance to initiate the handshake … step forward when he proffers his hand … on your left foot and into his personal space … this should force him to lean back and you'll be able to manipulate his hand into a more standard upright position … maybe even turn it fully over so you become the dominant party. If this doesn't work and he remains palm down, just grab him by the wrist … place your hand on top of his. Though that might be considered a little aggressive. It's up to you.

BORIS: Are we certain he's even in the country?

NIKOLAI: He's at the hotel.

BORIS: Our hotel?

IIVO: He has a three room suite.

BORIS: Have you seen him?

IIVO: No … one of the Icelanders said.

BORIS: I thought they were giving him a house in the suburbs?

NIKOLAI: Wasn't to his liking.

BORIS: I'm not going to grab him by his wrist.

GUÐMUNDUR enters.

EFIM: Okay … they're ready.

The Russian team ready themselves to enter the arena.

GUÐMUNDUR: Um … if you could just … wait … one moment …

NIKOLAI: What is it?

EFIM: He's not here.

GUÐMUNDUR: No … we're still … we'll hold the ceremony … only … it looks like it won't be Fischer drawing the pieces with you.

EFIM: [I knew it.]

BORIS: What does that mean?

IIVO: Is he here? Is he in the building?

GUÐMUNDUR: He's in Reykjavík.

NIKOLAI: But he's not coming to the ceremony?

GUÐMUNDUR: He's sent a substitute in his place … his second … William Lombardy.

BORIS: How is he allowed to do that?

GUÐMUNDUR: There's no rule that says that he can't. The drawing ceremony is largely … ceremonial. *(Beat.)* What should I …? Will you … will you go on?

NIKOLAI: Could you give us a moment …?

GUÐMUNDUR: Guðmundur.

NIKOLAI: Guðmundur. Thank you.

GUÐMUNDUR: Of course. *(Exits.)*

BORIS: It's a direct and deliberate insult.

IIVO: So rise above it and ...

BORIS: This isn't a schoolyard. He's not cussing out my mother. It's calculated. Am I wrong?

EFIM: No.

IIVO: No ... but you should not take it as a ...

BORIS: *I* am not insulted ... he doesn't insult *me* ...

EFIM: He insults the Soviet people.

BORIS: To send an underling in his place ...

NIKOLAI: And Father Lombardy at that.

IIVO: Why is that significant?

BORIS: Because I've played Lombardy before ... and he beat me. Twelve years ago.

NIKOLAI: You were cocky.

BORIS: And he was better. Then.

EFIM: What would you have us do?

BORIS: I don't know.

EFIM: Demand an apology ... demand a forfeit of the first game ... of the tournament?

BORIS: I do not know.

EFIM: Do we leave? Do you want us to leave?

BORIS: I want Fischer to be a human being.

EFIM: Do you want to call Moscow?

BORIS: No.

NIKOLAI: We are too concerned with his motives. Whether he's a narcissist or a tactician … it doesn't ultimately matter. He wants to elicit a reaction … whether that's to gain an advantage or simply because he craves the attention … either way we must be the adults in the room.

IIVO: You should ask for an apology at least.

NIKOLAI: But as a disappointed parent, not a fuming enemy.

EFIM: Boris …?

BORIS: Fine.

GUÐMUNDUR enters.

GUÐMUNDUR: Gentlemen …? We are ready for you.

Laugardalshöll arena.

The drawing ceremony.

An elevated stage. A wooden table and two chairs – one chair is wooden and upholstered in yellow, the other is a black leather swivel chair. A chessboard. A chess clock. Television cameras.

MAX and LOTHAR are onstage. LOTHAR holds a small bag.

BORIS enters from one side. WILLIAM LOMBARDY from the other. They meet in the middle and shake hands. LOTHAR opens the bag. BORIS and WILLIAM reach inside and draw a piece each. They reveal the colour of their pieces. BORIS's is white and WILLIAM's is black.

Much applause.

5.

Laugardalshöll arena.

The same elevated stage. BOBBY is inspecting the space. FRED and GUÐMUNDUR stand to one side.

BOBBY: Brighter.

The lighting gets brighter.

BOBBY: Less.

The lighting dims.

BOBBY: Less.

The lighting dims again.

BOBBY: Brighter.

The lighting gets brighter.

BOBBY: Less.

The lighting dims fractionally.

BOBBY: Better.

GUÐMUNDUR: Let's set the level there.

BOBBY: Brighter.

The lighting gets brighter.

GUÐMUNDUR: There?

BOBBY: *(Nods.)*

GUÐMUNDUR: *(Icelandic – 'Okay … let's set it there.'.)* Ókei …
höfum þetta svona.

BOBBY: The front row is too close. Remove the front two
rows.

GUÐMUNDUR: We have sold tickets for …

BOBBY: Move them back or take them out.

GUÐMUNDUR: We'll see if we can move them back.

BOBBY: No … no … just get rid of them … breathing down
my neck.

FRED: You should be writing this down.

GUÐMUNDUR: Everything meets with the pre-agreed
specifications.

FRED: Specifications can change.

GUÐMUNDUR: Of course, but … this is … this is …

BOBBY: *(Swivels in his chair.)*

GUÐMUNDUR: Charles Eames for the Time-Life building in
New York. We had it flown out especially.

FRED: It's a good-looking chair.

GUÐMUNDUR: It is.

BOBBY: *(Swivels the full 360 degrees.)*

FRED: Bobby?

BOBBY: I like the chair. The cameras need to move back.

GUÐMUNDUR: The cameras have been placed for optimal broadcast quality.

BOBBY: *(Inspects the pieces on the chessboard.)*

GUÐMUNDUR: *(Looks at his watch.)*

FRED: Are we keeping you up?

GUÐMUNDUR: Not at all.

BOBBY: *(Weighing one of the pieces in his hand.)* Lead weighted?

GUÐMUNDUR: Yes.

BOBBY: The pieces are fine but I don't like the board … too much pattern in the stone … too many spots … flecks.

GUÐMUNDUR: There have been weeks of consultation … weeks to manufacture …

BOBBY: Have another one made.

GUÐMUNDUR: We cannot delay for the sake of the board!

FRED: No one is suggesting a delay.

GUÐMUNDUR: Requesting a new board is tantamount to …!

FRED: How long would it take?

GUÐMUNDUR: I'm not a stonemason.

FRED: Perhaps you should talk to one.

GUÐMUNDUR: This was commissioned specifically.

FRED: Commission another.

GUÐMUNDUR: Now?!

FRED: Why not?

GUÐMUNDUR: It is two o'clock in the morning.

FRED: Do you require a break … for some dinner … or perhaps some coffee? Or do you want to speak to your stonemason?

BOBBY: The table needs to be an inch lower.

GUÐMUNDUR: I need to make some calls.

GAME ONE

SPASSKY (WHITE) vs FISCHER (BLACK)

NIMZO-INDIAN

1.d4 Nf6 2.c4 e6 3.Nf3 d5 4.Nc3 Bb4 5.e3 0-0 6.Bd3 c5
7.0-0 Nc6 8.a3 Ba5 9.Ne2 dxc4 10.Bxc4 Bb6 11.dxc5
Qxd1 12.Rxd1 Bxc5 13.b4 Be7 14.Bb2 Bd7 15.Rac1
Rfd8 16.Ned4 Nxd4 17.Nxd4 Ba4 18.Bb3 Bxb3 19.Nxb3
Rxd1+ 20.Rxd1 Rc8 21.Kf1 Kf8 22.Ke2 Ne4 23.Rc1 Rxc1
24.Bxc1 f6 25.Na5 Nd6 26.Kd3 Bd8 27.Nc4 Bc7 28.Nxd6
Bxd6 29.b5 Bxh2 30.g3 h5 31.Ke2 h4 32.Kf3 Ke7 33.Kg2
hxg3 34.fxg3 Bxg3 35.Kxg3 Kd6 36.a4 Kd5 37.Ba3 Ke4
38.Bc5 a6 39.b6 f5 40.Kh4 f4 41.exf4 Kxf4 42.Kh5 Kf5
43.Be3 Ke4 44.Bf2 Kf5 45.Bh4 e5 46.Bg5 e4 47.Be3 Kf6
48.Kg4 Ke5 49.Kg5 Kd5 50.Kf5 a5 51.Bf2 g5 52.Kxg5 Kc4
53.Kf5 Kb4 54.Kxe4 Kxa4 55.Kd5 Kb5 56.Kd6

BOBBY resigns. BORIS wins.

BORIS SPASSKY (USSR)

1

ROBERT FISCHER (USA)

0

GAME TWO

FISCHER (WHITE) vs SPASSKY (BLACK)

FISCHER does not show.

Forfeit. BORIS wins.

BORIS SPASSKY (USSR)

2

ROBERT FISCHER (USA)

0

6.

The Loftleiðir Hotel, Reykjavík.

The restaurant is empty but for BOBBY and LINA GRUMETTE.

BOBBY is tucking into a big bowl of ice cream.

LINA: The way it is being reported … dear me …

BOBBY: What are they saying?

LINA: Oh … unnecessary things.

BOBBY: Like?

LINA: Enough for me to buy a plane ticket.

BOBBY: I haven't read them.

LINA: Best that you don't.

BOBBY: Okay. *(Beat.)* What do they say?

LINA: It's the darnedest thing ... and strikes me as decidedly
un-American ...

BOBBY: What are they saying?

LINA: Oh, ignore the press, Bobby. I am here now ... that is
all that matters.

BOBBY: You want to watch a movie?

LINA: If that's what you want to do.

BOBBY: The hotel has a screening room.

LINA: If that's what you need. *(Beat.)* You're like a son to me,
Bobby.

BOBBY: What is it ... Hollywood to Reykjavík ... four
thousand miles?

LINA: Four and a half.

BOBBY: Must've been a long flight. *(Beat.)* Spassky says that I
have insulted the Soviet people. Good. They're due a few
insults. They should show respect.

LINA: How are they not showing you respect?

BOBBY: I have twenty successive wins behind me.
Grandmasters ... former world champions ...

LINA: But not Spassky.

BOBBY: They do not want me to win.

LINA: Why would any opponent want you to win?

BOBBY: Because I am the better player.

LINA: You must prove it.

BOBBY: I don't have to prove anything.

LINA: The World Championship must be won. It is not simply bestowed.

BOBBY: I am the better player.

LINA: Not if you leave. Not if you pick up your ball and go home.

BOBBY: I play the game. The Soviets play the rules and conventions of the World Chess Federation. I will not run from Spassky ... I will play Spassky ... bring him here ... set up the board and pieces ... I will show him who is the world champion.

LINA: Then why not play in the arena?

BOBBY: Because I might not win.

LINA: Bobby ... my dearest, Bobby ... I believe in you.

BOBBY: Do you think I lack in confidence? Have you ever known me lack the confidence? No. If I play, then they can cheat.

LINA: How?

BOBBY: The whole Soviet machine is an unfair advantage.

LINA: It is not cheating to invest in a national sport ... a national pastime.

BOBBY: I've not been funded. And I wouldn't take it.

LINA: And so your chess is purer?

BOBBY: Yes.

LINA: You've played Spassky before ... and you have never won.

BOBBY: He cheats.

LINA: Bobby …

BOBBY: They are in cahoots … all of the Russian players. They throw games … they go soft on each other … they manipulate the rankings. A Russian plays a Russian and there's no fight … no struggle … because who wins and who loses is decided in the Kremlin long before the game actually begins.

LINA: Then why partake in something so corrupt?

BOBBY: It is the World Championship. It is my title by rights.

LINA: Not until you win it.

BOBBY: For as long as I am the best player in the world. *(Beat.)* The lights are too bright. The audience is too close.

LINA: You worry too much about that sort of thing.

BOBBY: I want the purest game.

LINA: The game is not the board. Or rather the board is not just the board. It is the table … the chair … the arena … the audience … the morning's news … your opponent's relationship with his wife … his breakfast … your breakfast … it is every game … every circumstance in which he has won … or lost … as it is all of your victories and all of your failures. The board does not end … and the game began long before either of you ever met.

BOBBY: I am the better player.

LINA: So you say.

BOBBY: Did you bring what I asked for?

LINA: Yes. You want them now?

BOBBY: Yes.

LINA: *(Gets a stack of comics out of her bag.)*

BOBBY: *(Looks through the comics – Tarzan, Superman.)*

LINA: Are those the right ones?

BOBBY: *(Nods.)*

LINA: Tarzan.

BOBBY: Yes.

LINA: Superman.

BOBBY: Yes.

LINA: How long have we known each other, Bobby?

BOBBY: Since I was seventeen.

LINA: Twelve years. A chess club is nothing without its resident wunderkind. You will miss it. You think you will not. You think the label 'child prodigy' patronises you. You will be judged as a man in this contest. Not as a curiosity … not as a savant. I wonder how much that scares you.

BOBBY: I am not scared.

LINA: No?

BOBBY: No.

LINA: Many would call you scared. Many would read your actions as those of a frightened child.

BOBBY: *(Furious.)*

LINA: Go ahead … stamp your feet … throw a tantrum. No one will see. No one will know but your Lina. You could have called a draw. Spassky would've accepted.

BOBBY: No.

LINA: *(Looks at the comics.)* A lord raised by apes. An alien god raised by corn-belt yokels. *(Beat.)* How is your mother? She must be proud.

BOBBY: She doesn't matter. *(Beat.)* Do you know who is on his team?

LINA: Who?

BOBBY: Nikolai Krogius … Iivo Nei … Efim Geller.

LINA: I know Krogius. I know Geller.

BOBBY: Efim Geller is a Jew.

LINA: What are you going to do?

BOBBY: I don't like the cameras. They make me feel sick.

LINA: How so?

BOBBY: The closeness of them. I want to get on a plane.

LINA: You want to run away.

BOBBY: It would be a boycott. It would be a protest.

LINA: It would be running away.

BOBBY: I know Henry Kissinger.

LINA: You do?

BOBBY: He calls me on the telephone.

LINA: He wants you to win. All anyone wants is for you to do what you do best. Everyone is going out of their way to make you feel at home.

BOBBY: Homes can be dirty. Homes can be boring. I like hotels.

LINA: The Russians won't want to win by default. The Icelanders have over-invested. Henry Kissinger is on the phone. The game has never been bigger. That you were willing to throw away the second game … it gives weight to your threats … it shows them that you are not bluffing. You have never been in a stronger position.

BOBBY: I won't go back into that arena.

LINA: The game is not the arena. *You* are the game.

BOBBY: *(Nods.)*

LINA: So you will stay?

BOBBY: *(Nods.)*

LINA: I want to hear you say it.

BOBBY: I will stay.

LINA: Good. Have you finished your ice cream?

BOBBY: Yes. Thank you.

LINA: Now … tell me … what movie should we watch?

7.

The Loftleiðir Hotel.

BORIS, EFIM, IIVO and NIKOLAI – a chessboard in the middle of the room.

EFIM: It's a broom-cupboard.

NIKOLAI: It's not a broom-cupboard.

EFIM: Fischer wants to hold the World Championship in a broom-cupboard.

IIVO: It is currently set up for table tennis.

NIKOLAI: The Federation has agreed in principle.

EFIM: His number one complaint is of the noise levels in the arena … the distraction. This alternative room backs onto a main road! It's a joke.

NIKOLAI: It's not about the noise … it's about control.

BORIS: It makes no difference to me. I can play with frozen fingers and an empty stomach … I can play in a cupboard.

EFIM: You shouldn't have to.

NIKOLAI: He's trying to dispense with the ceremony … the trappings of the occasion.

EFIM: I get that. How can we use it?

NIKOLAI: We can keep him uncomfortable. Discomfort makes him petulant … makes him bratty.

EFIM: You have the move list for the first game?

IIVO: Of course. *(Finds his notebook.)*

EFIM: Set up move 29.

BORIS: We're in the middle of a game.

EFIM: *(Takes IIVO's notebook and starts rearranging the pieces.)*

IIVO: At least let me make a note of …

EFIM: You were going to lose.

BORIS: We'll play again later.

EFIM: Fischer's move … Bishop to h2.

BORIS: His Bishop is trapped … he can take two pawns only …

NIKOLAI: You were playing for the draw.

IIVO: Maybe he wasn't expecting you to do that.

EFIM: It's more that he doesn't respect it.

31

NIKOLAI: He's not interested in being forced into a stalemate.

BORIS: Is he purposefully throwing the game …?

EFIM: He thinks winning on points is as bad as losing. He's looking for the knockout. Let's assume the mistake was planned.

NIKOLAI: We can't assume anything.

EFIM: For the sake of argument. The 'mistake' was planned … the forfeiture … the cupboard … it is all planned. So if we subvert his will … if we demand to play the arena … with cameras, with audience … what has he gained? Distraction? Unnecessary negotiation? Deflection? Maybe he wants to exhaust us mentally with all his bullshit.

BORIS: It's working. *(To IIVO.)* Smoke a cigarette with me.

IIVO: *(Produces a pack of cigarettes.)* These ones have a little camel on the packet.

BORIS: *(Amused.)*

NIKOLAI: You should go to bed.

BORIS: I haven't eaten.

NIKOLAI: We'll order room-service.

BORIS: I'm not hungry.

NIKOLAI: Go next door. Lie down. Order yourself some room service. Eat some food.

EFIM: Bishop to h2. And the forfeit … in the forfeited game he was playing white … he would've opened with the advantage …

IIVO: He wants to …

EFIM: It shouldn't matter what he *wants*. It's the moves ... the moves not the man. His moves are stronger in the middle and end games ... but his openings are predictable. Open with the Queen's pawn and he'll play a King's Indian defence. He thinks himself a radical, so beat him where he's most conservative.

BORIS: What strategies have we got for King's Indian?

NIKOLAI: We can work on that.

BORIS: I won't sleep.

NIKOLAI: Stare at the ceiling ... watch television ... have a bath. Turn off your chess brain.

BORIS: I might go for a swim.

NIKOLAI: Good. Do it. We'll crunch strategy and let you know what results.

BORIS: *(Nods and exits.)*

Silence.

IIVO: Have you ever played table tennis?

NIKOLAI: It is not a serious pursuit.

EFIM: 'Ping-pong'.

IIVO: *(To EFIM.)* They have a table downstairs – if you fancy a game?

EFIM: I think I'll leave it to the Chinese.

IIVO: Why do they invest in table tennis of all things?

NIKOLAI: They want to be seen as swift, precise, skilled ... and the best propaganda for that is to lead the world in table tennis. Russia has marked as its territory chess, ballet and circus. Chess is the intellect ... ballet the art ... and circus is gymnastic, physical prowess. This is how we choose to lead – in brain, heart and body.

IIVO: Chess doesn't strike me as an especially Soviet game. If the pawns would take their own castles … overthrow their bishops … drag the king and queen to the cellar and shoot them in the face, then maybe …

EFIM: Iivo …

IIVO: What? I'd say the same at home.

EFIM: But of course you would, Comrade.

IIVO: And the Americans? What do they invest in?

NIKOLAI: Hollywood. They are the world leaders in escapism. They are the kings of Fantasyland. I think we are happy enough to cede that territory. Boris isn't playing a grandmaster; he's facing a movie-star. *(Beat.)* Fischer is testing his boundaries … like a tiger in a new enclosure … like a horse in a field … but he's not getting the pushback he expected … the fence isn't electrified after all … the checks and balances of the Chess Federation are, in the end, hollow threats.

EFIM: He's waiting for someone to say 'no'.

IIVO: So we say 'no'. We say 'play in the arena in the proper manner'.

NIKOLAI: And be seen as the rigid, inflexible, Politburo automatons they already believe us to be? He's a 'maverick' … a freewheeling, rule-breaking, *Easy Rider*. If we win by enforcing the rules, we lose.

IIVO: *(Starts resetting the board.)* I have some ideas on how we should approach a King's Indian …

NIKOLAI: Why don't you go and join Boris? He's exhausted. Keep him from drowning.

EFIM: We can handle this.

IIVO: If you think that's where I'll be of most use. Why don't I just show you ...?

EFIM: You're a sparring partner, not a strategist. Leave this to us.

IIVO: *(Nods, exits.)*

EFIM and NIKOLAI sit down at the board and are quickly immersed in strategy.

8.

Laugardalshöll arena.

The back room.

The table, chairs and board have been reset here.

GUÐMUNDUR is up a ladder. He is wrapping a blanket around a small CCTV camera mounted high in a corner.

LOTHAR paces around the room.

GUÐMUNDUR: Can you hear that?

LOTHAR: No.

GUÐMUNDUR: Good.

LOTHAR: I couldn't hear it before.

GUÐMUNDUR: What does it look like?

LOTHAR: Like you've wrapped a camera in a blanket.

GUÐMUNDUR: I need to check the feed ... make sure it's not obscuring ... do you think he will notice?

LOTHAR: Are you trying to camouflage ...?

35

GUÐMUNDUR: No, just dampen any sound … or perhaps …
the magnetic field. Should I wrap the camera in plastic?

LOTHAR: Would that do anything?

GUÐMUNDUR: I am not a scientist.

LOTHAR: Neither is Fischer.

GUÐMUNDUR: Tinfoil?

BORIS enters. LOTHAR shakes his hand.

BORIS: We are all set?

LOTHAR: I hope so.

GUÐMUNDUR: The clock is due to start at 5pm.

BORIS: Thank you.

*GUÐMUNDUR takes his ladder and goes. BORIS looks up at the
CCTV camera.*

LOTHAR: There are a thousand people in the arena. We have
set up a screen. And one in the press lounge.

BORIS: *(Waves at the camera.)*

LOTHAR: It is not broadcasting yet.

BORIS sits at the table.

*LOTHAR opens a window. The noise of traffic and children playing
bleeds in from outside.*

LOTHAR: Does that bother you?

BORIS: *(Shakes his head.)*

LOTHAR: Thank you.

BORIS: I wonder what you will concede to him next? Perhaps
I will have to come dressed as a clown.

Silence.

LOTHAR: How are you finding your hotel?

BOBBY enters. LOTHAR proffers a hand. BOBBY ignores him. He looks up at the camera.

BOBBY: 'Removed' – do you understand the word?

LOTHAR: Yes, but ...

BOBBY: I want the cameras removed.

LOTHAR: As per your request, there is only one remaining camera ...

BOBBY: That was not my 'request' ... I asked for *no* cameras ...

LOTHAR: ... and so we compromise with one.

BOBBY: You tell me the cameras are removed ... they are not removed ... therefore you are a liar and I cannot deal with you.

LOTHAR: It is out of your eye-line ... it is hidden from ...

BOBBY: I can hear it ... I can feel it ...

LOTHAR: There is no discernible ... detectable ... difference in the decibel level of ...

BOBBY: Your machines are faulty ... if they cannot detect what I can clearly hear ... what use are they?

LOTHAR: I am telling you that there is no difference between the cameras being present and not.

BOBBY: When electricity runs through a wire an electromagnetic field is created.

LOTHAR: I really don't think ...

BOBBY: Do you deny this?

LOTHAR: Perhaps if Comrade Spassky was complaining of something similar …

BOBBY: That is not likely.

LOTHAR: We are not removing the camera.

BOBBY: I call bullshit. I call corruption. The Chess Federation is a Communist front.

LOTHAR: We have commitments … we have contracts … broadcast rights … television …

BOBBY: I do not care about television. I am the reason people are watching.

LOTHAR: I thought you wanted the money?

BOBBY: I want what is mine. I want what is due.

LOTHAR: Deals have been made. I am not going to renege on … it is not making any noise … no noise at all …

BOBBY: Shut up.

LOTHAR: Bobby …

BOBBY: *(Spits on LOTHAR.)*

LOTHAR: *(Shocked, wipes the saliva from his face.)*

BORIS: *(Stands.)*

LOTHAR: *(Motions for BORIS to sit.)*

BOBBY: Don't look at him … look at me.

LOTHAR: Bobby … please …

BORIS: [This is insane.]

LOTHAR: … one second … please …

BORIS: I am returning to my hotel. When I return ... *if* I return ... it will be to the arena as agreed and as is proper.

LOTHAR: There is no need for ...

BOBBY: If you move the game back into the arena, I will take a hammer and smash the board to pieces!

LOTHAR: Gentlemen ... please! Boris ... you made a promise ... to play in this room. Bobby ... you must be kind. No one wants another forfeited game ... sit ... come and sit ... Boris ... will you sit?

BORIS sits.

LOTHAR: Bobby ... sit ... please ...

LOTHAR leads BOBBY to the table. He sits.

GUÐMUNDUR enters.

GUÐMUNDUR: Are we ready to begin?

LOTHAR: Gentlemen?

GUÐMUNDUR: Whenever you are ready.

GAME THREE

SPASSKY (WHITE) vs FISCHER (BLACK)

MODERN BENONI

1.d4 Nf6 2.c4 e6 3.Nf3 c5 4.d5 exd5 5.cxd5 d6 6.Nc3 g6 7.Nd2 Nbd7 8.e4 Bg7 9.Be2 0-0 10.0-0 Re8 11.Qc2 Nh5 12.Bxh5 gxh5 13.Nc4 Ne5 14.Ne3 Qh4 15.Bd2 Ng4 16.Nxg4 hxg4 17.Bf4 Qf6 18.g3 Bd7 19.a4 b6 20.Rfe1 a6 21.Re2 b5 22.Rae1 Qg6 23.b3 Re7 24.Qd3 Rb8 25.axb5 axb5 26.b4 c4 27.Qd2 Rbe8 28.Re3 h5 29.R3e2 Kh7 30.Re3 Kg8 31.R3e2 Bxc3 32.Qxc3 Rxe4 33.Rxe4 Rxe4

34.Rxe4 Qxe4 35.Bh6 Qg6 36.Bc1 Qb1 37.Kf1 Bf5
38.Ke2 Qe4+ 39.Qe3 Qc2+ 40.Qd2 Qb3 41.Qd4 Bd3+

BORIS resigns. BOBBY wins.

BORIS SPASSKY (USSR)
2
ROBERT FISCHER (USA)
1

9.

The Loftleiðir Hotel.

EFIM, NIKOLAI and IIVO around a chessboard.

IIVO: Boris opens with d4.

EFIM: Fischer plays Knight f6 … and we think we're in for
a King's Indian opening … because … because that's
what Fischer plays … has always played … and Boris is
prepared … has practiced for this …

IIVO: Boris follows with his pawn to c4.

EFIM: But Fischer doesn't want to do that … he plays e6 …

IIVO: Boris responds with Knight f3 …

EFIM: … and we're no longer in King's Indian … we're
playing Modern Benoni.

IIVO: It's not in Fisher's top ten.

EFIM: It's not in his repertoire.

NIKOLAI: He gets a reputation for playing King's Indian
… spends his entire career playing King's Indian … his

opponent studies King's Indian … so when he reaches the World Championship he plays Modern Benoni … a sequence of moves he's never been known to play before … a once-in-a-career manoeuvre. Bobby Fischer has been playing this game his entire life.

IIVO: People don't think that far in advance.

NIKOLAI: Maybe *you* don't.

EFIM: We have to throw out all of our books … our notes … everything we thought we understood about him as a player …

IIVO: Look at move eleven … Knight to h5 … no one plays like that.

EFIM: He's hugging the sides … he attacks the centre from the sides.

NIKOLAI: One of the first things we learn is that to dominate the game you must control the four central squares …

EFIM: He's not just breaking the rules … any fool child can do that … he has spent his life mastering technique in order to now disassemble it. He's won. If we play him at the board … he's won.

IIVO: I think we should resist buying into his messiah complex. Boris is still leading by two games to one.

NIKOLAI: It only takes one bad game. All of us are only one bad game away from ruin.

EFIM: We need to get him back in the arena.

BORIS enters.

BORIS: I know I played poorly.

NIKOLAI: I wouldn't say that.

BORIS: It's as though we are playing by different rules.

IIVO: The knight is still the knight … the rook is still the rook
…

BORIS: He is at war with us.

NIKOLAI: Maybe.

BORIS: I am not a soldier.

NIKOLAI: No one's asking you to be.

BORIS: Have you spoken to the Kremlin recently? *(Beat.)* I
am not a political man. I have no desire to be a political
man.

EFIM: The times we live in don't allow for that.

BORIS: No, but … *chess* … dear gods of politics, leave me my
chess! *(Beat.)* He yelled at Lothar Schmid … he spat at
him … he told him to shut up.

IIVO: When was this?

BORIS: Before the game. I should've walked … I should've
stood up and left … a letter to the Federation and the first
flight to Moscow.

NIKOLAI: Why didn't you?

BORIS: I wanted to play.

IIVO: You can't claim a forfeit now.

BORIS: I don't want to claim a forfeit.

EFIM: This is such a fucking debacle.

BORIS: Put this board away. I can't look at it. *(Beat.)* He's a
boy really … and all boys need boundaries … but the
poor little fucker is brilliant, so we're all too scared to
tell him 'no'. I doubt he even knows what he represents

... what *this* represents ... the whole thing ... he is America ... I am Russia ... but I am a poor emissary for Communism. I am not even a Party member.

NIKOLAI: And you think Fischer is a good example of Americanism?

EFIM: He is ruthless ... self-obsessed ... paranoid ...

BORIS: I can only represent myself.

NIKOLAI: You do not get to choose what you represent.

BORIS: So I am to be paraded around like Gagarin ... Nureyev ... Pavlichenko ...?

NIKOLAI: You think you won't be put on a stamp if you win? Pavlichenko ... she and her rifle had to claim 309 Nazi scalps for that honour. You need only claim one American.

BORIS: I'm still ahead.

EFIM: Yes.

BORIS: Two games out of three.

EFIM: No one's saying you're not doing well.

BORIS: I'm done accommodating his theatrics.

NIKOLAI: Sure. We get the cameras back ... get the front rows reinstated ...

BORIS: The cameras aren't part of the game.

NIKOLAI: They really are.

BORIS: I don't want to win by tricks.

EFIM: There are no prizes for sportsmanship.

NIKOLAI: Do you think he won't be trying to keep you off balance?

BORIS: Perhaps we should kidnap his dog ... threaten to wring its neck ... that'll distract him.

NIKOLAI: I'm not saying that.

IIVO: I don't think I'd be okay with killing a dog.

EFIM: No one's asking you to.

NIKOLAI: What you want from him ... an honest game ... he will not give it to you.

BORIS: Then why am I even playing him at all?

NIKOLAI: Because his dishonest game cannot be seen to win.

IIVO: What breed is it?

EFIM: What?

IIVO: His dog? What breed? If we're going to kill it ...

BORIS: Why would that make a difference?

IIVO: I'm not sure.

NIKOLAI: He doesn't have a dog!

EFIM: I'll draft a letter to Lothar Schmid. Plain ... but forceful ... put the tournament back in the arena ... return to the conventions of championship play.

IIVO: They may not go for it.

EFIM: Of course they will.

IIVO: They want to keep Fischer onside.

BORIS: Stop it ... stop it ... this is nonsense.

NIKOLAI: Boris ...

BORIS: I am not going to buy into Fischer's self-created mythos. He is a man-baby with a startling aptitude – nothing more. He is so intimidated by the whole thing that he hides in his hotel room. Yet he is also so monumentally arrogant that he demands to relocate the World Championship to a broom-cupboard … and we cave … the FIDE caves. He demands that we treat him as some special case. No. No games but chess. Understood?

10.

In the countryside outside of Reykjavík.

BOBBY is chasing a sheep. SÆMUNDUR 'SÆMI-ROKK' PÁLSSON, a policeman, is watching.

BOBBY: They can run fast … faster than you think …!

SÆMI-ROKK: And jump.

BOBBY: Yes!

SÆMI-ROKK: Good at jumping. Good at landing.

BOBBY: Stupid animals.

SÆMI-ROKK: I don't think so.

BOBBY: They are. They are stupid.

SÆMI-ROKK: Not as smart as pigs or dogs maybe …

BOBBY: One turns left; they all turn left.

SÆMI-ROKK: Safety in numbers.

BOBBY: *(Shrugs.)*

SÆMI-ROKK: You want to go back to the hotel?

BOBBY: No.

SÆMI-ROKK: It is getting late.

BOBBY: What time is it?

SÆMI-ROKK: Nearly one.

BOBBY: In the morning?

SÆMI-ROKK: Yes.

BOBBY: The sun is up.

SÆMI-ROKK: Barely.

BOBBY: This country is a joke.

SÆMI-ROKK: We are not responsible for the sun. Your jumper is too thin.

BOBBY: I will run around if I am cold.

SÆMI-ROKK: I have a coat in my car.

BOBBY: You are not my mother.

SÆMI-ROKK: You want me to leave?

BOBBY: I did not ask for a bodyguard.

SÆMI-ROKK: I am not that.

BOBBY: I did not request a security detail.

SÆMI-ROKK: I am just here to be of help.

BOBBY: Who are you working for?

SÆMI-ROKK: Reykjavík Police.

BOBBY: Yes, but … who else?

SÆMI-ROKK: No one else.

BOBBY: The Chess Federation?

SÆMI-ROKK: No.

BOBBY: FBI ... CIA ... KGB ...?

SÆMI-ROKK: You think I am a spy?

BOBBY: You could be. Why not?

SÆMI-ROKK: I don't own a tuxedo.

BOBBY: What is your name again?

SÆMI-ROKK: Sæmundur Pálsson. Everyone calls me Sæmi-Rokk.

BOBBY: Why?

SÆMI-ROKK: I am a good dancer.

BOBBY: Sammy. Okay, Sammy. You play chess?

SÆMI-ROKK: Yes, but ...

BOBBY: But ...?

SÆMI-ROKK: I'm not going to play you.

BOBBY: But you do play?

SÆMI-ROKK: It is not my game. I know the rules, sure ... I am Icelandic ... the winters are long ... six months of the year is dark. When we're not having sex or making music, we play chess. It passes the time. But no ... I was never any good.

BOBBY: No?

SÆMI-ROKK: No.

BOBBY: What is your game?

SÆMI-ROKK: Handball. I was goalkeeper in the national team.

BOBBY: We don't have handball in New York. We have
baseball … football …

SÆMI-ROKK: Handball is like football … but with hands.

BOBBY: We use our hands in football.

SÆMI-ROKK: Well, that makes no sense.

BOBBY: What else?

SÆMI-ROKK: I do judo.

BOBBY: Judo?

SÆMI-ROKK: I am a gold medal winner in the Icelandic
championship.

BOBBY: Show me some.

SÆMI-ROKK: I'm not going to do that.

BOBBY: Show me some judo.

SÆMI-ROKK: No.

BOBBY: Throw me on the ground.

SÆMI-ROKK: What if I broke your arm … your fingers …
how would you play? The Icelandic economy would
collapse. I would be charged with treason.

BOBBY: I could refuse to play until you demonstrated some
judo.

SÆMI-ROKK: You would not do that.

BOBBY: No?

SÆMI-ROKK: I cannot tell if you are joking. *(Takes up a judo
stance.)* Stand here … like this … hands here and here …
okay?

BOBBY: Okay.

SÆMI-ROKK: Ready?

BOBBY: Yes.

SÆMI-ROKK: I am going to throw you to the ground.

BOBBY: Do it already!

SÆMI-ROKK: I can't.

BOBBY: Do it!

SÆMI-ROKK: *(Sweeps BOBBY's legs from under him and deposits him on the ground.)* There you go … judo.

BOBBY: You use these moves on criminals?

SÆMI-ROKK: I could do.

BOBBY: Have you though?

SÆMI-ROKK: We shouldn't be chasing sheep.

BOBBY: Do you like movies?

SÆMI-ROKK: I do. I like James Bond … *Thunderball … On Her Majesty's Secret Service …*

BOBBY: Not for me.

SÆMI-ROKK: That is a shame.

BOBBY: *Planet of the Apes.*

SÆMI-ROKK: Those are good films.

BOBBY: We are going to be friends.

SÆMI-ROKK: Okay.

BOBBY: Bobby and Sammy.

SÆMI-ROKK: If you like.

BOBBY: Can I ask you something … as a friend?

SÆMI-ROKK: Of course.

BOBBY: Do you think I've broken him?

SÆMI-ROKK: Spassky?

BOBBY: Of course Boris Spassky – who else?

SÆMI-ROKK: I thought perhaps you meant the sheep?

BOBBY: *(Laughs – much to his surprise.)*

SÆMI-ROKK: I could not say if he is broken, but you definitively won that last game.

BOBBY: Yeah … I don't care about that.

SÆMI-ROKK: You do not play to win?

BOBBY: No.

SÆMI-ROKK: That will come as a surprise to … everyone … the entire chess community.

BOBBY: *(Scoffs.)* 'Community'.

SÆMI-ROKK: For someone who is not trying to win, you seem to be doing very well for yourself.

BOBBY: I play so that I don't lose.

SÆMI-ROKK: Is that different?

BOBBY: Yes.

SÆMI-ROKK: It is subtle.

BOBBY: It is a distinct difference.

SÆMI-ROKK: Okay.

BOBBY: Winning is fine … very nice … good. But losing is a devastation. I play so that I don't lose. And I don't lose when the other guy is toast. The moment when you break someone … when you break their ego … I like that. You see their confidence wither. You take their bravado from them … their mask … and you see them for the nothing they are … and they see it too … they see themselves for the first time. Play me at chess and I will reveal your true self. *(Beat.)* The only Bond movie I've seen is *From Russia with Love.*

SÆMI-ROKK: It is a good one. You like it because of the chess?

BOBBY: I didn't say that I liked it. The chess scene is wrong. They based the board on Spassky versus Bronstein, Leningrad 1960. Only they removed pawns on c5 and d4 … which might have been better for the camera … better for the shot … but it made a nonsense of the game.

SÆMI-ROKK: How many games are there … in the tournament?

BOBBY: Best of twenty-four.

SÆMI-ROKK: You've a way to go yet then. Are you all the same … playing not to lose?

BOBBY: Are who all the same?

SÆMI-ROKK: Chess players.

BOBBY: I am not one of them. They don't matter.

SÆMI-ROKK: You are not a chess player?

BOBBY: Not in the way that they are. It is a cabal. They do not respect me.

SÆMI-ROKK: You are playing the world championship … you are the hero of chess.

BOBBY: No. Had I been a musical prodigy … with violin or piano … they would respect the work. They would respect the hours. Had I been proficient at football ... at baseball ... that would be best ... that would be welcome ... because it would confirm that the poor man is the working man ... the physical man ... the grunt labour. But chess is a sport of the brain ... of the intellect ... and these assholes like to equate intellect with education. So a poor boy from the Bronx must be dismissed as a savant ... a freak ... a curiosity. A horse who counts out to ten with his hoof. A parrot that greets you 'good morning'. Parade me like the dog-faced boy. Parade me like the gimps and the geeks and the bearded lady. 'Remarkable', they say, 'extraordinary'. But never as an equal. Never as a brother. So it is not enough to beat them. It is not enough to be counted among them. You must destroy them. There is no room in their world for you. So you must supersede their world. You must be so far above them that their world is nothing but dirt in the grooves of your shoe. Fuck them. Fuck their established structure. *(Beat.)* I'm going to get that sheep.

SÆMI-ROKK: Okay.

BOBBY: Are you going to help?

SÆMI-ROKK: Okay.

GAME FOUR

FISCHER (WHITE) vs SPASSKY (BLACK)

SICILIAN SOZIN

1.e4 c5 2.Nf3 d6 3.d4 cxd4 4.Nxd4 Nf6 5.Nc3 Nc6 6.Bc4 e6 7.Bb3 Be7 8.Be3 0-0 9.0-0 a6 10.f4 Nxd4 11.Bxd4 b5 12.a3 Bb7 13.Qd3 a5 14.e5 dxe5 15.fxe5 Nd7 16.Nxb5 Nc5 17.Bxc5 Bxc5+ 18.Kh1 Qg5 19.Qe2 Rad8 20.Rad1 Rxd1 21.Rxd1 h5 22.Nd6 Ba8 23.Bc4 h4 24.h3 Be3 25.Qg4 Qxe5 26.Qxh4 g5 27.Qg4 Bc5 28.Nb5 Kg7

29.Nd4 Rh8 30.Nf3 Bxf3 31.Qxf3 Bd6 32.Qc3 Qxc3
33.bxc3 Be5 34.Rd7 Kf6 35.Kg1 Bxc3 36.Be2 Be5 37.Kf1
Rc8 38.Bh5 Rc7 39.Rxc7 Bxc7 40.a4 Ke7 41.Ke2 f5
42.Kd3 Be5 43.c4 Kd6 44.Bf7 Bg3 45.c5+

Draw.

GAME FIVE

SPASSKY (WHITE) vs FISCHER (BLACK)

NIMZO-INDIAN

1.d4 Nf6 2.c4 e6 3.Nc3 Bb4 4.Nf3 c5 5.e3 Nc6 6.Bd3
Bxc3+ 7.bxc3 d6 8.e4 e5 9.d5 Ne7 10.Nh4 h6 11.f4 Ng6
12.Nxg6 fxg6 13.fxe5 dxe5 14.Be3 b6 15.0-0 0-0 16.a4 a5
17.Rb1 Bd7 18.Rb2 Rb8 19.Rbf2 Qe7 20.Bc2 g5 21.Bd2
Qe8 22.Be1 Qg6 23.Qd3 Nh5 24.Rxf8+ Rxf8 25.Rxf8+
Kxf8 26.Bd1 Nf4 27.Qc2 Bxa4

BORIS resigns. BOBBY wins.

GAME SIX

FISCHER (WHITE) vs SPASSKY (BLACK)

QUEEN'S GAMBIT DECLINED, TARTAKOWER

1.c4 e6 2.Nf3 d5 3.d4 Nf6 4.Nc3 Be7 5.Bg5 0-0 6.e3 h6
7.Bh4 b6 8.cxd5 Nxd5 9.Bxe7 Qxe7 10.Nxd5 exd5 11.Rc1
Be6 12.Qa4 c5 13.Qa3 Rc8 14.Bb5 a6 15.dxc5 bxc5 16.0-0
Ra7 17.Be2 Nd7 18.Nd4 Qf8 19.Nxe6 fxe6 20.e4 d4 21.f4
Qe7 22.e5 Rb8 23.Bc4 Kh8 24.Qh3 Nf8 25.b3 a5 26.f5
exf5 27.Rxf5 Nh7 28.Rcf1 Qd8 29.Qg3 Re7 30.h4 Rbb7
31.e6 Rbc7 32.Qe5 Qe8 33.a4 Qd8 34.R1f2 Qe8 35.R2f3
Qd8 36.Bd3 Qe8 37.Qe4 Nf6 38.Rxf6 gxf6 39.Rxf6 Kg8
40.Bc4 Kh8 41.Qf4

BORIS resigns. BOBBY wins. BORIS applauds.

BORIS SPASSKY (USSR)

2.5

ROBERT FISCHER (USA)

3.5

11.

Laugardalshöll arena.

The elevated stage.

The arena is empty.

A large wooden crate has been delivered.

MAX and GUÐMUNDUR inspect it.

MAX: When did it arrive?

GUÐMUNDUR: An hour ago.

MAX: Who placed the order?

GUÐMUNDUR: The Russians.

MAX: Has Fischer got wind of this?

GUÐMUNDUR: I don't know.

MAX: *(Heavy sigh.)*

GUÐMUNDUR: With all the concessions afforded to …

MAX: Can we get this open?

GUÐMUNDUR: Efim Geller has gone in search of a crowbar. *(Beat.)* There is no rule that says that they can't …

MAX: I know the rulebook. I am the rulebook.

GUÐMUNDUR: If we send it away, the Russians might …

MAX: The Russians won't do anything.

GUÐMUNDUR: They have threatened to withdraw from the Chess Federation …

MAX: That won't happen.

GUÐMUNDUR: Hmm.

MAX: What?

GUÐMUNDUR: Nothing … it's just … when the Americans threaten the same …

MAX: The threats are not equally weighted. The Americans have never won the championship – so they lose nothing if they walk. The Soviets, however, are invested to the tune of twenty-six years and ten titles. They can threaten and pout as much as they like but they know and I know that to denounce the Federation would invalidate … or worse diminish … the titles they historically hold. So no, I do not need to consider the Russians' feelings … and

yes, I will bend rules to accommodate the Americans
... because to the world Bobby Fischer is already the
champion. For America to walk and Fischer to not claim
his crown, well ... that would rather diminish us. *(Beat.)* I
apologise. This is all very unusual ... he is unusual ... and
we must not pretend otherwise.

GUÐMUNDUR: I just worry for our neutrality ... our
impartiality ...

MAX: Yes, yes ... all very nice ... as everyone abandons us
... as the televisions are turned off ... once they have all
gone home ... in our insignificance ... our neutrality will
be a soothing cup of cocoa. I played him ... fifteen years
ago ... in New York. He was just a boy ... a child ... and
I saw something of myself in him. I know what it is to
be a prodigy ... a curiosity. I saw a chance to teach him
the lesson I wish someone had taught me at that age. I
brought my full weight to a friendly game. I humiliated
him. He ran from the Manhattan Chess Club in tears.
A fourteen-year-old ... tall ... a man-looking child ...
bawling like a toddler. The next time we met ... three
years later ... he dispatched me easily ... as he would
today. He had become 'chess-sensation Bobby Fischer'.
He had earned it ... that payback ... with the unseen grind
that makes the virtuoso. If you are looking for genius,
that is where you'll find it ... everything else is just show-
business.

FRED enters.

FRED: This is outrageous.

MAX: Mr Cramer ...

FRED: This is a direct violation of our agreement ... we must
be consulted on any change to the set-up ... especially
regards to the staging area ...

MAX: There is nothing to say that a player cannot request an alternative …

FRED: It is unacceptable that Mister Fischer has no right of veto to any alteration to any item within the arena.

MAX: This is Comrade Spassky's space as much as it is Fischer's. We have changed the board at Bobby's request … we have made alterations to the table … to the proximity of the pot-plants …

FRED: … and the Russians could have rejected any of those if they so wished.

MAX: Fred … please … don't demean yourself.

EFIM and IIVO enter. EFIM is carrying a crowbar.

MAX: Are these games really necessary?

EFIM: Comrade Spassky has requested a new chair.

IIVO: He finds his current one too restrictive.

MAX: *(To FRED.)* Do you have any objections to Spassky replacing his chair?

FRED: I will have to consult with my team.

EFIM and IIVO break open the crate.

EFIM: I am sure Mister Fischer will find no cause for complaint.

The new chair revealed. It is exactly the same make and model as FISCHER's swivel-chair.

FRED: What is this?

EFIM: Spassky's new chair.

FRED: It's a replica …

EFIM: It's the same design.

FRED: We object.

IIVO: It's the same chair.

FRED: We object!

IIVO: What possible objection could you …?

FRED: There is no way he will stand for it.

IIVO: … could he possibly have to us using the exact same type of …?

FRED: Max …

EFIM: If it's good enough for the Americans, it's good enough for us.

FRED: You think you are so clever … so smart. It's an obvious attempt to …

IIVO: … to what?

EFIM: If anything it's a flattery.

FRED: How am I supposed to sell this to him?

IIVO: Comrade Spassky admired the chair. He admired its swivel.

EFIM: We are within our rights and within championship norms to replace our chair should we so desire. And we do. We do desire it.

FRED: This is a blatant attempt to unsettle …

IIVO: After all Fischer has done!

MAX: Honestly, Fred, no. What would you have me do? *(Beat.)* The longer you leave it before you tell him …

FRED: *(Nods.)*

EFIM: *(Grins.)*

FRED: You needn't look so smug, you piece of shit.

FRED heads to the exit, but at the last moment, decides to turn and rush the stage. He grabs onto the new chair and seeks to drag it from the arena. He is physically restrained by GUÐMUNDUR, IIVO and MAX.

12.

Naval Air Station Keflavik.

A US airbase thirty miles Southwest of Reykjavík.

A bowling alley.

BOBBY, SÆMI-ROKK and WILLIAM LOMBARDY are bowling.

A table with burgers, fries and milkshakes. WILLIAM has a pocket chessboard set up and is playing a game against himself in between throws.

WILLIAM: … and Benjamin Franklin responds: 'I see that my king is in check, but I won't defend him. Had he been a good king such as yours then he would deserve the protection of his subjects … but no … this king is a tyrant and has cost them more than he is worth. Take him, if you please … I can do without him … and I will fight out the rest of the game as a republic.'

SÆMI-ROKK: If you start changing the rules then you are no longer playing the same game.

WILLIAM: The game is manmade … the rules are manmade … and can be unmade or remade as man sees fit.

SÆMI-ROKK: But there must be agreement.

WILLIAM: If there are rules then there is ambiguity ... if there is ambiguity then we need interpretation.

SÆMI-ROKK: So speaks a man of God.

WILLIAM: What gave it away?

SÆMI-ROKK: The dog collar.

WILLIAM: I was joking.

SÆMI-ROKK: So was I.

WILLIAM: Right.

BOBBY: Talk about something else.

SÆMI-ROKK: Sorry.

BOBBY: *(Bowls.)*

WILLIAM: Bobby and I don't necessarily agree on religious matters. For example, I – as a Roman Catholic – believe in papal infallibility and transubstantiation. Bobby – as a member of Southern California's Worldwide Church of God – believes that Jesus will return to us perched on the back of a nuclear warhead.

SÆMI-ROKK: *(To BOBBY.)* You believe this?

BOBBY: I find it interesting.

SÆMI-ROKK: *(Bowls.)*

WILLIAM: We try not to talk about religion.

SÆMI-ROKK: When is this supposed to happen ... Jesus ... the second coming ... nuclear apocalypse?

BOBBY: 1975.

WILLIAM: Three years to go. Tick tock tick tock. I guess we'll just have to wait and see.

BOBBY: *(Steps up to the lane.)*

SÆMI-ROKK: Oh … Bobby … I think it's Father Lombardy's turn …

WILLIAM: *(Shakes his head to say: it doesn't matter.)*

BOBBY: *(Bowls.)*

SÆMI-ROKK: *(Bowls.)*

WILLIAM: *(Steps up to the lane.)*

BOBBY: *(Studying WILLIAM's chessboard.)* That's a mistake.

WILLIAM: Hmm?

BOBBY: You're sacrificing your pawn to no good advantage.

WILLIAM: I'm trying something. Leave me alone. *(Bowls.)* Are you a religious man, Mr Palsson?

SÆMI-ROKK: *(Shrugs.)* I'm a Protestant if I am anything.

BOBBY: *(The chessboard.)* If you put pressure on the black rook you'll force your opponent into a mistake.

WILLIAM: I am playing against myself.

BOBBY: Then you're going to lose. *(Bowls.)*

BOBBY is not very good at bowling.

SÆMI-ROKK: Here … let me show you … *(Takes a bowling ball and takes up a stance at the lane.)* It's all about your approach and position … you want your front foot in line with that central dot … two inches back from the foul line … approach from about five steps back … keep your centre of gravity low and …

BOBBY: It doesn't matter.

SÆMI-ROKK: What doesn't?

BOBBY: Approach … stance … position …

SÆMI-ROKK: I'm just showing you … if you want to avoid the gutter …

BOBBY: I don't care about the gutter.

SÆMI-ROKK: … if you want to strike the pins …

BOBBY: I throw this heavy ball to exercise my arm … so that I am in better physical shape … so that I am physically exercised … so that I may raise my heart rate … so that I may sleep deeper … so that I can play better chess. I'm not interested in strikes or spares or gutters … I am not interested in the pins at all. I'm done. Drive me to the hotel.

WILLIAM: We're supposed to be analysing Spassky's openings.

BOBBY: It doesn't matter.

WILLIAM: You've had a good run, but Boris knows how to win a tournament.

BOBBY: No. I sit with him at the table and you can see … it's gone … in his eyes … it's gone. I've broken him. But you're right in that I'm not quite finished … I still need to humiliate him.

WILLIAM: At least let's discuss strategy for five minutes.

BOBBY: Bill – you play like a house. What have you got to teach me?

WILLIAM: Unlike you I've actually won against Boris Spassky.

BOBBY: Do you think you'd win against him today?

WILLIAM: *(He knows he wouldn't.)*

BOBBY: Sammy – let's go.

WILLIAM: I am your second ... your support ... use me
  ... bounce ideas off me ... I am a resource ... and I am
  the closest you have to an equal in the American game.
  Spassky likes to sacrifice ... he likes to throw away a piece
  to no discernible advantage ... just to derail his opponent
  ... you know this ... so let's talk about it ... let's talk about
  how not to be distracted ...

BOBBY: I doubt he'll be in a state to deploy psychology.

WILLIAM: A few days ago, you were cowering in your room
  like a frightened child.

BOBBY: *(Furious.)* I am not a child!

WILLIAM: Oh so it's some 'master strategy'? That nonsense
  may fly in the papers, but not with those who know you
  ... those of us who see your hands shake.

BOBBY: I don't believe in psychology – I believe in good
  moves.

WILLIAM: Then show me.

BOBBY: *(Picks up a bishop from WILLIAM's board.)* What is this
  piece called?

WILLIAM: Excuse me?

BOBBY: What is this piece called?

WILLIAM: It's a bishop.

BOBBY: How does it move?

WILLIAM: You know how it moves.

BOBBY: Tell me.

WILLIAM: Diagonally.

BOBBY: *(Picks another piece from the board.)* And this?

WILLIAM: A rook.

BOBBY: And how does it move?

WILLIAM: *(Stubborn silence.)*

BOBBY: *(Throws pieces at WILLIAM.)* If you're going to treat me like a novice, treat me like a fucking novice.

WILLIAM: Calm down.

BOBBY: Suck my dick.

SÆMI-ROKK: The man's a priest ...

WILLIAM: It's alright ...

BOBBY: ... then he's a puppet. Puppets and vampires ... feeding off my energy ... scratching around for that reflected glory ... junkies twitching for it ... or it's fingers in all things ... levers and strings ... are you my shadow-man ... reporting to your elders ... your cabal ... whose familiar are you? You're a joke. I've made you, William Lombardy. I've fucking made you.

Silence.

WILLIAM: Mr Palsson ...?

SÆMI-ROKK: Yes, Father.

WILLIAM: Will you ensure he takes a bath tonight?

BOBBY: Stop it.

WILLIAM: Lay out a fresh suit and a clean shirt for tomorrow.

BOBBY: I told you to stop it.

WILLIAM: Encourage him to put a brush through his hair. He is representing America on the world stage.

BOBBY: I only represent myself.

WILLIAM: It's laughable if you believe that.

BOBBY: *(Upends the table.)*

WILLIAM: *(Calm.)*

BOBBY: *(Fuming.)*

SÆMI-ROKK: *(Begins to tidy.)*

WILLIAM: Why don't you wait for Bobby in the car, Mr Palsson?

SÆMI-ROKK: *(Exits.)*

WILLIAM: There was a time when I beat you at every game ... week in week out ... we'd sit down at the board ... Jack Collins' house ... and I would trounce you. We came up together ... those quiet rooms in the clubs in the brownstones ... the old Jewish men in the parks. You were twelve years old ... I was eighteen. Those old men ... they played you for the curiosity ... for the novelty. Did I ever play you for the novelty?

BOBBY: No.

WILLIAM: No, I did not. And though I won those games ... I never toyed with you ... I never patronised you ... I never treated you as a child. And then one day you simply 'got good' and I haven't beaten you since.

BOBBY: I know it.

WILLIAM: He dines out on that now ... 'Jack Collins: Svengali of Chess' ... mentor to Lombardy and Fischer ... but honestly, we were both well beyond his ability before we put one foot through his door. I bet you my last dime he's loving this ... watching you on TV ... the coverage in the Times ... 'the man who taught Bobby Fischer' ... 'taught him everything he knows' ...

BOBBY: *(Scoffs.)*

WILLIAM: We all have our teachers. You were one of mine.
I think I can say I was one of yours. So let's put away
this bullshit, please. You may well win ... you may well
argue that you have already won ... but if you think that
'good moves' alone will humiliate him, you have not paid
enough attention to your opponent. He applauded his
own defeat. He stood at the end of the sixth game and
applauded the beauty of what you had given him. To
defeat Spassky ... *truly* defeat him ... you must make it
ugly ... you must make the sight of the board repulsive
to him ... you must take what he loves and ruin it. Is that
what you want?

BOBBY: Yes.

WILLIAM: Good ... because it is what your country requires.
Collegial sportsmanship and fair play will win you
handshakes and backslaps ... but slaughter him ... offer
up his eviscerated corpse to the gods of war, and you will
be held aloft ... anointed and revered. Your countrymen
will see themselves reflected in you. Everything they want
to believe about their exceptionalism ... their superiority
... the *rightness* of their ideology ... will be confirmed.

BOBBY: When I win it will be *my* victory ... not America's.

WILLIAM: You can't extricate yourself from what you
represent.

BOBBY: What I *represent* is that I am the greatest ranked
chessplayer that has ever lived. The concentration is
mine ... the work is mine ... the stamina is mine. I came
to the chessboard on my own ... found the problems in
the back pages of newspapers by myself. Lots of people
... Jack Collins ... you ... Lina ... even Spassky ... will
claim mentorship ... will claim some possession of my

achievements ... but the greatest games I have ever won were against Bobby Fischer. And you tell me that people want to siphon off my energy ... my *lifeforce* ... for the pathetic coincidence that we happen to share a nationality? I did not decide the borders ... I did not issue the passports ... I do not recognise any kind of fellowship with you or with anyone.

WILLIAM: I am proud ... is that wrong of me? We are all so very proud of you.

BOBBY: Your pride is an insult. Reflected glory is theft. The Russians cheat. They have a hundred men in the Kremlin sweating and calculating and feeding back Spassky's moves. My moves are my own. My successes are my own. I will defeat him because I choose to ... and it will be a blow to their collectivism ... to their *communalism* ... good ... because I detest it. It will not be America that bloodies the Soviets' nose ... this is not America versus Russia ... this is Bobby Fischer versus all you fucks.

FRED enters – nervous.

WILLIAM: Yes?

FRED: They have ...

WILLIAM: Yes?

FRED: They have replaced Spassky's chair.

WILLIAM and FRED look at BOBBY – bracing themselves for his response.

FISCHER laughs and laughs and laughs.

GAME SEVEN

SPASSKY (WHITE) vs FISCHER (BLACK)

SICILIAN NAJDOF

DRAW

1.e4 c5 2.Nf3 d6 3.d4 cxd4 4.Nxd4 Nf6 5.Nc3 a6 6.Bg5
e6 7.f4 Qb6 8.Qd2 Qxb2 9.Nb3 Qa3 10.Bd3 Be7 11.0-0
h6 12.Bh4 Nxe4 13.Nxe4 Bxh4 14.f5 exf5 15.Bb5+ axb5
16.Nxd6+ Kf8 17.Nxc8 Nc6 18.Nd6 Rd8 19.Nxb5 Qe7
20.Qf4 g6 21.a4 Bg5 22.Qc4 Be3+ 23.Kh1 f4 24.g3 g5
25.Rae1 Qb4 26.Qxb4+ Nxb4 27.Re2 Kg7 28.Na5 b6
29.Nc4 Nd5 30.Ncd6 Bc5 31.Nb7 Rc8 32.c4 Ne3 33.Rf3
Nxc4 34.gxf4 g4 35.Rd3 h5 36.h3 Na5 37.N7d6 Bxd6
38.Nxd6 Rc1+ 39.Kg2 Nc4 40.Ne8+ Kg6 41.h4 f6 42.Re6
Rc2+ 43.Kg1 Kf5 44.Ng7+ Kxf4 45.Rd4+ Kg3 46.Nf5+
Kf3 47.Ree4 Rc1+ 48.Kh2 Rc2+ 49.Kg1

*In an upset, the game is a draw. It is as good as a victory for BORIS.
BOBBY however is stunned. He is left alone on the stage as doubt
creeps in.*

BORIS SPASSKY (USSR)

3

ROBERT FISCHER (USA)

4

ACT TWO

1.

A bar in central Reykjavík.

MAX is nursing a drink.

GUÐMUNDUR approaches, drink in hand.

GUÐMUNDUR: Can I join you?

MAX: Sure.

GUÐMUNDUR: If you need some peace … I'd hate to
     interrupt a quiet moment …

MAX: Nonsense. Sit down.

GUÐMUNDUR: This is a bit of a risk, isn't it?

MAX: What is?

GUÐMUNDUR: Drinking in a pro-Fischer bar. If the Russians
     see you … bang goes your air of impartiality.

MAX: I hadn't noticed.

GUÐMUNDUR: There's a poster with his face right on the
     door.

MAX: I'll finish this and then find a Spassky bar and drink the
     same. Just to be fair.

GUÐMUNDUR: Good idea.

MAX: The chessboard is still not right. Two weeks into the
     tournament and we're still negotiating the chessboard.

GUÐMUNDUR: What's wrong with it?

MAX: The shading of the squares … not enough definition … too light or too dark, I forget which. Worse than the marble board, he says.

GUÐMUNDUR: This is the wooden board?

MAX: Yep.

GUÐMUNDUR: What are you going to do?

MAX: Do? Nothing.

GUÐMUNDUR: Are we going ahead?

MAX: Oh … yes … yes … Spassky put his foot down … any alteration to the equipment must be approved by both sides …

GUÐMUNDUR: And Fischer agreed?

MAX: Nothing's certain until he's sat at the board … and even then … *(Shrugs.)* He's lashing out … blaming his tools … blaming Spassky's new chair … anything but himself. *(Beat.)* The system we have … the rules and the conventions of the International Chess Federation … there's an assumption at the heart of our system that we would always be dealing with reasonable men. The norms and customs of championship play never accounted for bullies and madmen.

GUÐMUNDUR: He is an outlier … a once-in-a-generation player …

MAX: It is in the event of outliers that we have such safeguards. He is popular … and that makes chess popular … and my God aren't we delighted. Take away the cameras … take away the circus … take away his charisma … and would we bend? No. There were too many exceptions made … too many rules circumvented or bent all out of shape … just so that we could proceed. I should have claimed the first game forfeit. We should not have tolerated his requests … even if it meant defaulting the championship to the Soviets. The fallout would have been great … the investment lost … the profile squandered … the *embarrassment* … but, after it all, we would have maintained our integrity. We have long been a dying interest … niche … exclusive and exclusionary … for the sake of some attention … for the sake of column inches and relevance we've let this arsehole crap all over us.

GUÐMUNDUR: Chess will survive Bobby Fischer.

MAX: And all the arseholes of the future will be able to cite him as precedent. How will we enforce laws we've so publicly allowed to be broken?

GUÐMUNDUR: Spassky could still win.

MAX: Would it matter now?

GUÐMUNDUR: So … should we void it all … start again …?

MAX: To what end?

GUÐMUNDUR: To restore faith.

MAX: Faith doesn't break, it dies … and what is dead remains dead. Trust, however … we can rebuild trust … but that takes time and repentance.

GUÐMUNDUR: He is our Muhammad Ali … our James Dean … the membership books of clubs across the whole world are full of fresh ink … new names …

MAX: And so we should allow him free rein … declare Bobby Fischer untouchable?

GUÐMUNDUR: He is a genius.

MAX: It is a stupid term. 'Geniuses' do not appear fully formed like a star in the night sky … no … they are more the tallest sunflower in the field. We are bound by laws and strictures … canes and wires … but for some reason allow men like him to grow like weeds. Why do we believe 'genius' to be so fragile that we cannot ask it to behave? Urgh … oh … I am drunk.

GUÐMUNDUR: You still have to find a pro-Spassky bar.

MAX: No, I have to find my hotel. And there … there you are … my bias laid bare.

GUÐMUNDUR: No one expected the rules would ever need to be enforced … we have never seen a player like him before.

MAX: Which is exactly why I should have enforced them! And now those chess clubs you speak of are filling up with aspiring Bobby Fischers … a generation of them … God help us.

GAME EIGHT

FISCHER (WHITE) vs SPASSKY (BLACK)

ENGLISH SYMMETRICAL

BLACK RESIGNS

1.c4 c5 2.Nc3 Nc6 3.Nf3 Nf6 4.g3 g6 5.Bg2 Bg7 6.0-0 0-0 7.d4 cxd4 8.Nxd4 Nxd4 9.Qxd4 d6 10.Bg5 Be6 11.Qf4 Qa5 12.Rac1 Rab8 13.b3 Rfc8 14.Qd2 a6 15.Be3 b5 16.Ba7 bxc4 17.Bxb8 Rxb8 18.bxc4 Bxc4 19.Rfd1 Nd7 20.Nd5 Qxd2 21.Nxe7+ Kf8 22.Rxd2 Kxe7 23.Rxc4 Rb1+ 24.Bf1 Nc5 25.Kg2 a5 26.e4 Ba1 27.f4 f6 28.Re2 Ke6 29.Rec2 Bb2 30.Be2 h5 31.Rd2 Ba3 32.f5+ gxf5 33.exf5+ Ke5 34.Rcd4 Kxf5 35.Rd5+ Ke6 36.Rxd6+ Ke7 37.Rc6

BORIS resigns, BOBBY wins.

BORIS SPASSKY (USSR)

3

ROBERT FISCHER (USA)

5

GAME NINE

SPASSKY (WHITE) vs FISCHER (BLACK)

QUEEN'S GAMBIT DECLINED, SEMI TARRASCH

DRAW

1.d4 Nf6 2.c4 e6 3.Nf3 d5 4.Nc3 c5 5.cxd5 Nxd5 6.e4
Nxc3 7.bxc3 cxd4 8.cxd4 Nc6 9.Bc4 b5 10.Bd3 Bb4+
11.Bd2 Bxd2+ 12.Qxd2 a6 13.a4 0-0 14.Qc3 Bb7 15.axb5
axb5 16.0-0 Qb6 17.Rab1 b4 18.Qd2 Nxd4 19.Nxd4 Qxd4
20.Rxb4 Qd7 21.Qe3 Rfd8 22.Rfb1 Qxd3 23.Qxd3 Rxd3
24.Rxb7 g5 25.Rb8+ Rxb8 26.Rxb8+ Kg7 27.f3 Rd2
28.h4 h6 29.hxg5

BORIS SPASSKY (USSR)

3.5

ROBERT FISCHER (USA)

5.5

GAME TEN

FISCHER (WHITE) vs SPASSKY (BLACK)

RUY LOPEZ BREYER

BLACK RESIGNS

1.e4 e5 2.Nf3 Nc6 3.Bb5 a6 4.Ba4 Nf6 5.0-0 Be7 6.Re1
b5 7.Bb3 d6 8.c3 0-0 9.h3 Nb8 10.d4 Nbd7 11.Nbd2 Bb7

12.Bc2 Re8 13.b4 Bf8 14.a4 Nb6 15.a5 Nbd7 16.Bb2 Qb8
17.Rb1 c5 18.bxc5 dxc5 19.dxe5 Nxe5 20.Nxe5 Qxe5
21.c4 Qf4 22.Bxf6 Qxf6 23.cxb5 Red8 24.Qc1 Qc3 25.Nf3
Qxa5 26.Bb3 axb5 27.Qf4 Rd7 28.Ne5 Qc7 29.Rbd1 Re7
30.Bxf7+ Rxf7 31.Qxf7+ Qxf7 32.Nxf7 Bxe4 33.Rxe4
Kxf7 34.Rd7+ Kf6 35.Rb7 Ra1+ 36.Kh2 Bd6+ 37.g3 b4
38.Kg2 h5 39.Rb6 Rd1 40.Kf3 Kf7 41.Ke2 Rd5 42.f4 g6
43.g4 hxg4 44.hxg4 g5 45.f5 Be5 46.Rb5 Kf6 47.Rexb4
Bd4 48.Rb6+ Ke5 49.Kf3 Rd8 50.Rb8 Rd7 51.R4b7 Rd6
52.Rb6 Rd7 53.Rg6 Kd5 54.Rxg5 Be5 55.f6 Kd4 56.Rb1

BORIS resigns, BOBBY wins.

BORIS SPASSKY (USSR)
3.5
ROBERT FISCHER (USA)
6.5

2.

The Loftleiðir Hotel, Reykjavík.

BORIS is alone in a darkened room. A half-drunk glass of orange juice in front of him. He stares at the glass of juice.

NIKOLAI enters.

NIKOLAI: You're supposed to be sleeping.

BORIS: I'm too tired.

NIKOLAI: If you want to join us in the bar …

BORIS: I don't think so.

NIKOLAI: We've revisited each of the games … we have some
  notes … on your moves … on Fischer's …

BORIS: And your conclusion?

NIKOLAI: Come for a drink … see for yourself.

BORIS: Does this juice taste odd to you?

NIKOLAI: Is it not fresh?

BORIS: Taste it.

NIKOLAI: *(Does so.)*

BORIS: Well?

NIKOLAI: It tastes of orange juice.

BORIS: *(Not satisfied.)*

NIKOLAI: What do you want me to say?

BORIS: Is there any juice in the minibar?

NIKOLAI: Come and have a drink … it'll help you relax.

BORIS: I don't want to relax. I want to compare this juice with the juice from the minibar.

NIKOLAI: Boris …

BORIS: What?

NIKOLAI: You're exhausted.

BORIS: I can't sleep.

NIKOLAI: We need to talk about your performance. You can barely sit up straight.

BORIS: I agree.

NIKOLAI: Great.

BORIS: But I don't think sleep will help. *(Opens a juice from the minibar and hands it to NIKOLAI.)*

NIKOLAI: Do you need to see a doctor?

BORIS: Drink it.

NIKOLAI: *(Does so.)*

BORIS: And now the other ...

NIKOLAI: *(Sips the original glass of juice.)*

BORIS: Well?

NIKOLAI: *(Shrugs.)*

BORIS: How does it taste?

NIKOLAI: What do you want me to ...?

BORIS: Just ... have an opinion.

NIKOLAI: This one's sour.

BORIS: It is.

NIKOLAI: You want me to complain to the hotel?

BORIS: I brought this one back from the arena.

NIKOLAI: So it's been at room temperature for five hours.

BORIS: It was sour before. Why do you think I brought it
back here?

NIKOLAI: I honestly have no idea.

BORIS: I'm fine at the hotel ... I'm awake ... I'm alert ...
psychologically prepped ... but when I sit at the board ...
I'm lethargic ... sluggish ... I can't focus ...

NIKOLAI: ... and you're blaming the caterers?

BORIS: Don't make light of this.

NIKOLAI: I'm not. You asked for fresh juice. But we are in
Iceland. How fresh can the oranges be?

BORIS: Do we trust the Americans not to spike my food?

NIKOLAI: *(Has no answer.)*

BORIS: Could I be playing better? Yes. Could I have been better prepared? Maybe. Would you expect the reigning world champion to struggle as I have these last few games? No. And I don't think that's me being arrogant.

NIKOLAI: I can't watch out for their dirty tricks … I'm not equipped to recognize them.

BORIS: I think they're poisoning me.

NIKOLAI: Bobby Fischer doesn't want to beat you poisoned … what kind of victory is that?

BORIS: It needn't come from Fischer. I wouldn't put it past Lombardy. I wouldn't put it past their crook of a president.

NIKOLAI: You shouldn't have been so belligerent back in Moscow … you should have accepted the offer of an interpreter … a fixer …

BORIS: I wasn't going to welcome the KGB on to my team.

NIKOLAI: *(Sigh.)*

BORIS: What?

NIKOLAI: You think the KGB are just going to stay at home … because you asked? *(Beat.)* Moscow has concerns. They've studied footage of you playing and want to sweep the arena for radiation … they're talking about maybe the Americans have used hypnosis … parapsychology …

BORIS: Mind-control?

NIKOLAI: … subconscious coercion … I don't know …

BORIS: Is that even possible?

NIKOLAI: *(Non-committal.)*

BORIS: Is that your opinion as a psychologist?

NIKOLAI: I'm guessing there's an element of projection here … 'We always see our own mistakes in our opponent.'

BORIS: I only ever wanted to play chess.

NIKOLAI: That last game …

BORIS: It was as though I had the flu.

NIKOLAI: He was aggressive … he played aggressively … and that affects rational thought. If you're forced to only think defensively … *(Beat.)* So maybe that's it … not poison or radiation or psy-ops.

BORIS: I played against Misha Tal … Tbilisi, 1965 … and Tal is friends with Wolf Messing …

NIKOLAI: The psychic?

BORIS: Mesmerist … telepathist … whatever he calls himself. I didn't know he was in the audience until after the game. I made mistakes … moves a novice wouldn't make. I froze for minutes at a time … as though my brain had short-circuited.

NIKOLAI: Do you think you were influenced by …?

BORIS: I was not in control of myself at that board.

NIKOLAI: And you feel that same way now?

BORIS: Yes … something similar, at least.

Silence.

NIKOLAI: I don't know how you screen an audience for telepaths.

BORIS: You are making fun of me.

NIKOLAI: I think you are looking for excuses. *(Beat.)* The Sports Committee have asked me to fly home.

BORIS: When?

NIKOLAI: Now. Today.

BORIS: Absolutely not. Why?

NIKOLAI: Because you're not winning. Because he is ahead by three games. And they want to know why.

BORIS: I can pull it back.

NIKOLAI: You should be doing better than you are.

BORIS: No. You can't go. Tell them I need you here.

NIKOLAI: Fine.

BORIS: Send them this juice. Bottle it up ... diplomatic bag it back to Moscow ... test it in a lab ...

NIKOLAI: ... and then what? If they find sedatives ... isotopes ... voodoo ... what do you think would happen?

BORIS: We would have proof!

NIKOLAI: So? It wouldn't matter. How they win doesn't matter. Cheating and lying and subterfuge is just a sideshow ... only really of interest to geeks and obsessives. The vast majority of people see it as all part of the larger game. The Cold War is still a war. Soft power is still power. You're out here playing by the rules ... they're out here playing to the crowd. *(Beat.)* I will send a sample of this to Moscow ... but it won't be your silver bullet. Be careful. You get a lot of leeway ... a lot of freedom ... as world champion.

BORIS: I've never been super-political ...

NIKOLAI: ... and the fact that that's permitted speaks volumes. You may not want to engage with this ... all of this ... the time you were born into ... the politics of the day ... you may consider yourself above such things ... as an artist-grandmaster ... as a world champion ... but, fucking hell, Boris ... try to be aware of your context.

BORIS: What should I be doing ... as a 'Good Soviet' ... as a 'Good Russian'? Should I speak of the glory of the Motherland? The weakness of the Western ways of life? Or maybe I should highlight the paranoia ... the fear we all live with ... the famines we try to forget? Or maybe I should mention the insane waste of resource that is our tit-for-tat pissing contest of a space race ... of an arms race? Perhaps I should talk of Baba Yaga and her grandson, the Devil, and how they squat hunched over in the Politburo ... at the ears of our leaders ... with their fingers in our lives and their nails at our throats.

NIKOLAI: You are going to lose the World Championship. To an American. Russian chess dominance will come to an end. Because of you. All of the perks and the freedoms that you currently enjoy ... all of the dispensations and the blind-eyes ... they'll be gone ... and you'll be back under the same scrutiny as the rest of us. I hope you're ready.

GAME ELEVEN

SPASSKY (WHITE) vs FISCHER (BLACK)

SICILIAN NAJDORF

BLACK RESIGNS

1.e4 c5 2.Nf3 d6 3.d4 cxd4 4.Nxd4 Nf6 5.Nc3 a6 6.Bg5 e6 7.f4 Qb6 8.Qd2 Qxb2 9.Nb3 Qa3 10.Bxf6 gxf6 11.Be2 h5 12.0-0 Nc6 13.Kh1 Bd7 14.Nb1 Qb4 15.Qe3 d5 16.exd5 Ne7 17.c4 Nf5 18.Qd3 h4 19.Bg4 Nd6 20.N1d2 f5 21.a3

Qb6 22.c5 Qb5 23.Qc3 fxg4 24.a4 h3 25.axb5 hxg2+
26.Kxg2 Rh3 27.Qf6 Nf5 28.c6 Bc8 29.dxe6 fxe6 30.Rfe1
Be7 31.Rxe6

BOBBY resigns, BORIS wins. It is shocking – a comeback.

BORIS SPASSKY (USSR)
4.5
ROBERT FISCHER (USA)
6.5

3.

The Loftleiðir Hotel – BOBBY's hotel room.

BOBBY is on the telephone to HENRY.

Celebratory noises bleed in from elsewhere in the hotel.

HENRY: Bobby …?

BOBBY: Wait.

HENRY: Bobby … are you there?

BOBBY: I'm here.

HENRY: What's happening, Bobby?

BOBBY: Can you hear that?

HENRY: I don't …

BOBBY: Noise.

HENRY: I can't hear anything, Bobby.

BOBBY: Listen. *(Beat.)* The Russians.

HENRY: What are they doing?

BOBBY: Cheering, I think … singing …

HENRY: A celebration?

BOBBY: They're taunting me … to keep me from my sleep.

HENRY: It's his first win for three weeks … it's to be expected. *(Beat.)* Everyone over here speaks very fondly of you. You are doing good things and we are proud. The American people want you to do well. You mustn't lose heart, Bobby … not over losing a single game.

BOBBY: He was lucky and I wasn't paying attention. He distracted me.

HENRY: How did he distract you?

BOBBY: I don't know … I don't know … but he must have done.

HENRY: You are still ahead.

BOBBY: They don't play fairly … they're arrogant and they don't show respect.

HENRY: And that is why it is important that you bring them down a peg or two. Would you like that? To bring them down a peg? You are ahead by a good margin. I have every faith that you will continue to lead and deliver a conclusive and devastating blow.

BOBBY: My mother's a Communist. Did you know that?

HENRY: *(Long pause.)* Yes, I did know that, Bobby.

BOBBY: She sent me to Moscow when I was fifteen … hoping that I'd get bitten by the 'red bug'. But I'm not so feeble-minded. I saw through them. I wanted to play Botvinnik … I wanted to play Smyslov … but I was told that they were unavailable. Grown men too scared to face me. I played Petrosian … you know Petrosian? He bored me to tears. The lesser players … they were lining up to play me … to be beaten by me … delighting in it like some pervert masochists. It was a joke. And when we were done I asked them … the Moscow Central Chess Club … 'where's my money?' 'You're a guest … we don't pay fees to guests!' They're herd animals … clumping together … relying on others to pick up after their mistakes … to clean the gravel from their grazes … to wipe their shitty asses. Not one of them could survive alone.

HENRY: You have your own team, Bobby. Father Lombardy …

BOBBY: He's a joke.

HENRY: And I am here … on the phone … talking to you. And you have the American people … they are your team. They have a great investment in you, Bobby … a great investment in your doing well.

BOBBY: I didn't ask for it and I don't want it.

HENRY: You are not alone in this. *(Pause.)* Who won … between you and Petrosian?

BOBBY: Why?

HENRY: I am curious.

BOBBY: He did … most of the time.

HENRY: Then I'm sure you must have learnt something. *(Beat.)* Do you know what my job is, Bobby?

BOBBY: You work for President Nixon.

HENRY: I *advise* President Nixon. Do you know on what matters I advise him?

BOBBY: *(Shrugs.)*

HENRY: Bobby … are you there?

BOBBY: I shrugged.

HENRY: This is a telephone call, Bobby … I can't see it if you shrug. *(Beat.)* My job is mostly concerned with foreign affairs … with America's standing in the world … our *engagement* with other governments and regimes. War. We are fighting a war right now. Do you know how the Vietnamese fight a war?

BOBBY: No.

HENRY: They exhaust us … they have us chasing after false targets. A guerrilla soldier wins when he does not lose. A conventional army loses when it does not win. Are you a guerrilla, Bobby?

BOBBY: *(No response.)*

HENRY: In all things there are rules that are written and rules that are not. A written rule is easier to bend or break because language is fallible … language is translatable … mutable. The words themselves hardly matter. But I always advise against breaking the *unwritten* rules … because breaking them can cause far more damage. Fairness … justice … betrayal – these are the rules I am talking about. Better to keep them moving … keep them undefined … never pin them down. Always be aggrieved.

BOBBY: Have you got what you wanted?

HENRY: How do you mean?

BOBBY: In your life.

HENRY: The problem is … is that I want a great deal.

BOBBY: There's an episode of *Star Trek* … the crew find this woman … her spaceship crashed on this planet years before … everyone aboard died but her … a child … her injuries were great ... and the aliens tried to put her back together ... tried to stitch her back together ... but they'd never seen a human before ... didn't know what one should look like ... didn't know what should go where. So she was a mangled, monstrous thing. How can you build something ... feel something ... *live* something ... if you've never seen it ... if you don't know what it's supposed to look like?

HENRY: I know you will do your country proud.

BOBBY: People say that like it should mean something. But I don't think I like America very much, Mister Kissinger.

HENRY: Is that so, Bobby?

BOBBY: It is.

HENRY: Can I ask why?

BOBBY: It's built on death. Nothing is earned ... everything is taken. Taken from the red man and built on the labour of the black ... and the working class whites buy into it ... keep the system as it is ... sustained by the false hope of the American Dream ... that uncashable IOU ... told that they are the best, shining example to the world ... even as they're forced to sit in their own shit.

HENRY: I don't think that is fair, Bobby.

BOBBY: Are you a Jew, Mister Kissinger?

HENRY: By birth, yes ... though I am sure there are those within the community who would disown me if they could. I am as Jewish as you are, Bobby.

BOBBY: I'm not even circumcised. *(Beat.)* Does your job cover ivory?

HENRY: Ivory?

BOBBY: The international trade in ivory.

HENRY: No … that would be the United States Fish and Wildlife Service. Why do you ask?

BOBBY: I want you to do something about the elephants.

HENRY: The elephants?

BOBBY: Yes.

HENRY: What's wrong with the elephants, Bobby?

BOBBY: They are being hunted to extinction.

HENRY: Yes. It's a … I'm sure it's a bad situation.

BOBBY: It's because an elephant's trunk reminds them of an uncircumcised penis.

HENRY: The Jews want to wipe out elephants because a trunk looks like a penis?

BOBBY: Yes.

HENRY: *(Laughs, long and hard.)*

BOBBY: Don't laugh at me. Stop laughing at me. I'm serious.

HENRY: Oh, Bobby Bobby Bobby … you're American but not American … Jewish but not Jewish … what does that leave?

BOBBY: *(Silence.)*

HENRY: Bobby …?

BOBBY: *(Silence.)*

HENRY: Are you there …?

BOBBY: *(Doesn't respond.)*

The sound of Russian drinking songs fills the hotel.

GAME TWELVE

FISCHER (WHITE) vs SPASSKY (BLACK)

QUEEN'S GAMBIT DECLINED, ORTHODOX

DRAW

1.c4 e6 2.Nf3 d5 3.d4 Nf6 4.Nc3 Be7 5.Bg5 h6 6.Bh4 0-0
7.e3 Nbd7 8.Rc1 c6 9.Bd3 dxc4 10.Bxc4 b5 11.Bd3 a6
12.a4 bxa4 13.Nxa4 Qa5 14.Nd2 Bb4 15.Nc3 c5 16.Nb3
Qd8 17.0-0 cxd4 18.Nxd4 Bb7 19.Be4 Qb8 20.Bg3 Qa7
21.Nc6 Bxc6 22.Bxc6 Rac8 23.Na4 Rfd8 24.Bf3 a5 25.Rc6
Rxc6 26.Bxc6 Rc8 27.Bf3 Qa6 28.h3 Qb5 29.Be2 Qc6
30.Bf3 Qb5 31.b3 Be7 32.Be2 Qb4 33.Ba6 Rc6 34.Bd3
Nc5 35.Qf3 Rc8 36.Nxc5 Bxc5 37.Rc1 Rd8 38.Bc4 Qd2
39.Rf1 Bb4 40.Bc7 Rd7 41.Qc6 Qc2 42.Be5 Rd2 43.Qa8+
Kh7 44.Bxf6 gxf6 45.Qf3 f5 46.g4 Qe4 47.Kg2 Kg6 48.Rc1
Ba3 49.Ra1 Bb4 50.Rc1 Be7 51.gxf5+ exf5 52.Re1 Rxf2+
53.Kxf2 Bh4+ 54.Ke2 Qxf3+ 55.Kxf3 Bxe1

BORIS SPASSKY (USSR)

5

ROBERT FISCHER (USA)

7

GAME THIRTEEN

SPASSKY (WHITE) vs FISCHER (BLACK)

ALEKHINE'S DEFENCE

WHITE RESIGNS

1.e4 Nf6 2.e5 Nd5 3.d4 d6 4.Nf3 g6 5.Bc4 Nb6 6.Bb3 Bg7
7.Nbd2 0-0 8.h3 a5 9.a4 dxe5 10.dxe5 Na6 11.0-0 Nc5
12.Qe2 Qe8 13.Ne4 Nbxa4 14.Bxa4 Nxa4 15.Re1 Nb6
16.Bd2 a4 17.Bg5 h6 18.Bh4 Bf5 19.g4 Be6 20.Nd4 Bc4

21.Qd2 Qd7 22.Rad1 Rfe8 23.f4 Bd5 24.Nc5 Qc8 25.Qc3
e6 26.Kh2 Nd7 27.Nd3 c5 28.Nb5 Qc6 29.Nd6 Qxd6
30.exd6 Bxc3 31.bxc3 f6 32.g5 hxg5 33.fxg5 f5 34.Bg3
Kf7 35.Ne5+ Nxe5 36.Bxe5 b5 37.Rf1 Rh8 38.Bf6 a3
39.Rf4 a2 40.c4 Bxc4 41.d7 Bd5 42.Kg3 Ra3+ 43.c3 Rha8
44.Rh4 e5 45.Rh7+ Ke6 46.Re7+ Kd6 47.Rxe5 Rxc3+
48.Kf2 Rc2+ 49.Ke1 Kxd7 50.Rexd5+ Kc6 51.Rd6+
Kb7 52.Rd7+ Ka6 53.R7d2 Rxd2 54.Kxd2 b4 55.h4
Kb5 56.h5 c4 57.Ra1 gxh5 58.g6 h4 59.g7 h3 60.Be7 Rg8
61.Bf8 h2 62.Kc2 Kc6 63.Rd1 b3+ 64.Kc3 h1=Q 65.Rxh1
Kd5 66.Kb2 f4 67.Rd1+ Ke4 68.Rc1 Kd3 69.Rd1+ Ke2
70.Rc1 f3 71.Bc5 Rxg7 72.Rxc4 Rd7 73.Re4+ Kf1 74.Bd4
f2

BORIS resigns, BOBBY wins.

BORIS SPASSKY (USSR)

5

ROBERT FISCHER (USA)

8

4.

Laugardalshöll arena.

*IIVO, EFIM, FRED and GUÐMUNDUR are on the elevated stage. BORIS
watches to one side.*

The lighting rig is lowered. GUÐMUNDUR inspects each lamp.

FRED: I don't know what you expect to find.

GUÐMUNDUR: And I don't know what I'm looking for.

EFIM: There will be some device … some machinery or
electronics that should not be there.

IIVO: Something that doesn't look right.

EFIM: There are frequencies that can cause nausea … can disrupt concentration … can incapacitate …

FRED: Are they kidding … are you kidding with this?

IIVO: What do you mean?

FRED: That's rich … that's really rich … don't give me this 'frequencies' crap … what do you take us for? When your own people sit in the front row blowing on whistles …!

IIVO: Who's blowing on whistles?

FRED: Don't try to deny it.

GUÐMUNDUR: A couple of Icelanders … members of the audience … reported a Russian man sitting in the front row with a thin metal tube between his lips. Anytime an official walked past he would retract the tube back into his mouth. We tried to follow it up, but we couldn't find him after the game.

IIVO: How did they know he was Russian?

GUÐMUNDUR: They overheard him talking.

EFIM: We know nothing of this.

FRED: Of course you would say that.

IIVO: During which game?

FRED: Excuse me?

IIVO: During which game was this supposed to have happened?

FRED: The tenth.

IIVO: I didn't hear a whistle.

FRED: Because the pitch was so high that it was inaudible.

IIVO: Then what would be the point in blowing it?!

FRED: Fischer suffers from hyperacusis.

IIVO: I don't know what that is.

FRED: It means he doesn't like whistles.

EFIM: He won the tenth.

FRED: What?

EFIM: Fischer won the tenth game.

FRED: So?

EFIM: So the whistle … if there was a whistle … which I doubt … didn't make the blindest bit of difference anyway.

FRED: That's not the point and you know it.

GUÐMUNDUR: Am I looking for a transmitter or a speaker or …?

IIVO: Something that emits radiation.

GUÐMUNDUR: And what does a 'radiation emitter' look like?

EFIM: Like it doesn't belong in a lighting rig.

GUÐMUNDUR: Wouldn't such a device affect the audience as well?

FRED: That's fair, isn't it? Shouldn't people be vomiting in the aisles?

GUÐMUNDUR: Or at least complaining of headaches or stomach upsets or …?

EFIM: We don't know how advanced this technology is … how directional … how *controlled* …

FRED: This is some Buck-Rogers-bullshit. You're trying to imagine into existence a technology to suit your paranoia.

IIVO: Searching this rig is in your interest just as much as it is in ours.

FRED: If your side had planted anything … then yes, I'm sure you would lead me directly to it and show me how it works.

GUÐMUNDUR: If the Russians were really cheating, you'd think they would have won a few more games by now.

The Soviets are not amused.

GUÐMUNDUR: Sorry.

EFIM: You're going too slowly. *(Starts inspecting the lamps himself.)*

GUÐMUNDUR: Wait! I've … I think I've …

EFIM: What is it?

GUÐMUNDUR: *(Inspecting a lamp.)* There's … hang on … there's something in here.

Everybody gathers round as GUÐMUNDUR opens up the lamp.

GUÐMUNDUR: Hang on … nearly there … nearly got it … two of them …

EFIM: What are they?

GUÐMUNDUR: Bugs.

EFIM: I knew it.

GUÐMUNDUR: Not *bugs* … not *spy-bugs.* They're flies … look … two of them.

EFIM: What?

GUÐMUNDUR: Two dead flies.

IIVO starts laughing. GUÐMUNDUR laughs as well. FRED joins in.

EFIM: Keep looking.

IIVO: Efim ... please ...

EFIM: Keep looking!

BORIS, quiet until now, strides over to the two chairs on the stage. He pulls at FISCHER's chair and upends it.

FRED: Hey! Woah! You can't ... you can't ...

GUÐMUNDUR: Mister Spassky ... Comrade Spassky ... please ...

BORIS: Open this up.

GUÐMUNDUR: No ... we can't tamper with ...

BORIS: Open up the chair! Take it apart!

FRED: What are you doing?!

BORIS: Fischer is getting external help ... a radio receiver ... a miniature computer ... something ... there is something in his chair and it reeks of corruption.

GUÐMUNDUR: Please ... there's no need for –

FRED: It is the responsibility of the Icelandic Chess Federation to ensure that there is no tampering with –

GUÐMUNDUR: Yes ... yes ... of course ... Comrade Spassky ... Boris ...

FRED: We will not tolerate Soviet interference with our *American* chairs.

GUÐMUNDUR: We can't pull it apart without any suggestion of ... without probable cause ... please.

EFIM: X-ray it.

GUÐMUNDUR: What?

EFIM: You have X-ray machines on this little island, don't you? X-ray it.

BORIS: Yes!

GUÐMUNDUR: Come on now ... this is ridiculous ...

BORIS: X-ray Fischer's chair or the entire Soviet team walks.

5.

In the countryside outside of Reykjavík.

SÆMI-ROKK and BOBBY.

SÆMI-ROKK: Raven-Flóki ... Hrafna-Flóki ... Flóki Vilgerðarson ... he was the first of the Norsemen to set sail for Iceland. Oh there had been rumours ... fables ... but Raven-Flóki was the first to seek it. He set sail from Horgaland, Norway ... sailed to Shetland and the Faroes ... before striking out west. He took with him three ravens. Ravens, as you'll know, are not seabirds – they will not land on water like gulls. Once the Faroes were behind him, Hrafna-Flóki released the first of the ravens. The bird flew straight up into the sky, and ... seeing nothing but the Faroes far behind them ... flew backwards from the stern for the safety of that little archipelago. Days past before Flóki thought to release the second raven. This one flew up, and ... seeing no land at all ... circled a few times before returning to the boat. Flóki and his men continued on. On the day he released the third raven it flew upwards from the boat ... but it didn't return ... no, it flew north-westerly ... straight on from the prow. Raven-Flóki steered his ship in the direction of his raven, knowing that it must've sighted land. Flóki and his men disembarked at what we now call Reykjavík ... a place where butter dripped from every blade of grass ... or so they said. I would like to have seen that Reykjavík ... this one is wet and grey and smells of fish. *(Beat.)* What you do not know ... and what I can see ... as I watch you eating your burgers and fries ... swimming in the hotel pool ... on the stage with Spassky ... what you do not know is that you are a raven. Where you go, the world is going to follow.

BOBBY: I am not a leader.

SÆMI-ROKK: Maybe not a politician or a general or a guru ... but you set precedence. You make space for others to act as you act ... to think as you think.

BOBBY: I am not responsible for anyone but myself.

SÆMI-ROKK: No. And neither is the raven.

BOBBY: I'm not interested in that.

SÆMI-ROKK: Of course you are not.

BOBBY: Ravens are scavengers.

SÆMI-ROKK: Yes they are.

BOBBY: I am not a scavenger.

SÆMI-ROKK: No.

BOBBY: I am the top of the food chain.

SÆMI-ROKK: Why does that matter? *(Pause.)* I am a policeman. I am a judo champion. If there is a domestic disturbance ... if there is a scuffle in a bar ... a fist-fight ... a punch-up ... I am there. And it always calms down when I arrive. If the uniform isn't enough ... if my height and build isn't enough ... then the reputation is. Sometimes a tough guy ... drunk ... tries his luck ...

throws a punch ... it is easily dealt with. Whatever the situation is, I can usually calm it. Judo hold or a night in the cells. These men have a constant need to jostle for the top in any situation ... I've never felt the need myself. All it takes is for a bigger dog to turn up. I am a big dog. I have become an expert in the insecurities of men.

BOBBY: You think I need a big boy to come and put me in my place? I've had my nose broken and my pocket change taken. I got over it.

SÆMI-ROKK: I think you worry that there are no bigger dogs than you ... and what would that mean? If you are the biggest dog and the world is *even then* still chaos, then it means we are all fucked. And this is where we find the paranoia ... the conspiracies ... the accusations of unfairness ... as if somehow you are being victimised even as you ascend to the throne. You have everything you say you want ... everything you have set out to achieve ... but you do not seem content. You seem horrified at a world that would glorify you.

BOBBY: Careful, Sammy.

Silence.

SÆMI-ROKK: There's going to be a new James Bond.

BOBBY: Is that so?

SÆMI-ROKK: Yes.

BOBBY: Who?

SÆMI-ROKK: Roger Moore.

BOBBY: I don't know who that is.

SÆMI-ROKK: Neither do I. *(Beat.)* I'm driving back into town. I can give you a lift or you can walk back alone. Which is it to be?

GAME FOURTEEN

FISCHER (WHITE) vs SPASSKY (BLACK)

QUEEN'S GAMBIT DECLINED, HARRWITZ

DRAW

1.c4 e6 2.Nf3 d5 3.d4 Nf6 4.Nc3 Be7 5.Bf4 0-0 6.e3 c5
7.dxc5 Nc6 8.cxd5 exd5 9.Be2 Bxc5 10.0-0 Be6 11.Rc1
Rc8 12.a3 h6 13.Bg3 Bb6 14.Ne5 Ne7 15.Na4 Ne4 16.Rxc8
Bxc8 17.Nf3 Bd7 18.Be5 Bxa4 19.Qxa4 Nc6 20.Bf4 Qf6
21.Bb5 Qxb2 22.Bxc6 Nc3 23.Qb4 Qxb4 24.axb4 bxc6
25.Be5 Nb5 26.Rc1 Rc8 27.Nd4 f6 28.Bxf6 Bxd4 29.Bxd4
Nxd4 30.exd4 Rb8 31.Rxc6 Rxb4 32.Kf1 Rxd4 33.Ra6
Kf7 34.Rxa7+ Kf6 35.Rd7 h5 36.Ke2 g5 37.Ke3 Re4+
38.Kd3 Ke6 39.Rg7 Kf6 40.Rd7 Ke6

BORIS SPASSKY (USSR)

5.5

ROBERT FISCHER (USA)

8.5

GAME FIFTEEN

SPASSKY (WHITE) vs FISCHER (BLACK)

SICILIAN NAJDORF

DRAW

1.e4 c5 2.Nf3 d6 3.d4 cxd4 4.Nxd4 Nf6 5.Nc3 a6 6.Bg5
e6 7.f4 Be7 8.Qf3 Qc7 9.0-0-0 Nbd7 10.Bd3 b5 11.Rhe1
Bb7 12.Qg3 0-0-0 13.Bxf6 Nxf6 14.Qxg7 Rdf8 15.Qg3
b4 16.Na4 Rhg8 17.Qf2 Nd7 18.Kb1 Kb8 19.c3 Nc5
20.Bc2 bxc3 21.Nxc3 Bf6 22.g3 h5 23.e5 dxe5 24.fxe5

Bh8 25.Nf3 Rd8 26.Rxd8+ Rxd8 27.Ng5 Bxe5 28.Qxf7
Rd7 29.Qxh5 Bxc3 30.bxc3 Qb6+ 31.Kc1 Qa5 32.Qh8+
Ka7 33.a4 Nd3+ 34.Bxd3 Rxd3 35.Kc2 Rd5 36.Re4 Rd8
37.Qg7 Qf5 38.Kb3 Qd5+ 39.Ka3 Qd2 40.Rb4 Qc1+
41.Rb2 Qa1+ 42.Ra2 Qc1+ 43.Rb2 Qa1+

BORIS SPASSKY (USSR)

6

ROBERT FISCHER (USA)

9

GAME SIXTEEN

FISCHER (WHITE) vs SPASSKY (BLACK)

RUY LOPEZ EXCHANGE

DRAW

1.e4 e5 2.Nf3 Nc6 3.Bb5 a6 4.Bxc6 dxc6 5.0-0 f6 6.d4 Bg4
7.dxe5 Qxd1 8.Rxd1 fxe5 9.Rd3 Bd6 10.Nbd2 Nf6 11.Nc4
Nxe4 12.Ncxe5 Bxf3 13.Nxf3 0-0 14.Be3 b5 15.c4 Rab8
16.Rc1 bxc4 17.Rd4 Rfe8 18.Nd2 Nxd2 19.Rxd2 Re4
20.g3 Be5 21.Rcc2 Kf7 22.Kg2 Rxb2 23.Kf3 c3 24.Kxe4
cxd2 25.Rxd2 Rb5 26.Rc2 Bd6 27.Rxc6 Ra5 28.Bf4
Ra4+ 29.Kf3 Ra3+ 30.Ke4 Rxa2 31.Bxd6 cxd6 32.Rxd6
Rxf2 33.Rxa6 Rxh2 34.Kf3 Rd2 35.Ra7+ Kf6 36.Ra6+
Ke7 37.Ra7+ Rd7 38.Ra2 Ke6 39.Kg2 Re7 40.Kh3 Kf6
41.Ra6+ Re6 42.Ra5 h6 43.Ra2 Kf5 44.Rf2+ Kg5 45.Rf7
g6 46.Rf4 h5 47.Rf3 Rf6 48.Ra3 Re6 49.Rf3 Re4 50.Ra3
Kh6 51.Ra6 Re5 52.Kh4 Re4+ 53.Kh3 Re7 54.Kh4 Re5
55.Rb6 Kg7 56.Rb4 Kh6 57.Rb6 Re1 58.Kh3 Rh1+
59.Kg2 Ra1 60.Kh3 Ra4

BORIS SPASSKY (USSR)

6.5

ROBERT FISCHER (USA)

9.5

6.

The Loftleiðir Hotel – a hotel room.

EFIM and NIKOLAI. NIKOLAI is holding an X-ray.

NIKOLAI: I'm not about to accuse the Americans of espionage.

EFIM: Why not … if they're guilty of it?

NIKOLAI: This makes things worse, not better … do you understand that?

EFIM: We are in the right and they are in the wrong.

NIKOLAI: *(Pointing to something on the X-ray.)* You can't even tell me what this object does.

EFIM: I'm not a spy … I don't know spy-craft. I'm not familiar with gadgets and technology … of what is or what is not possible in the realms and worlds of espionage … telephones in shoe heels … tracking devices in cigarette packets … but this is quite clearly … *something.*

NIKOLAI: Unless I have been briefed to do so, I won't start hurling around accusations. This is an international stage covered by the international press.

EFIM: There is no bad time to expose a cheat … a fraud … a hypocrite.

NIKOLAI: Boris may have said that he didn't want to be chaperoned, but do you honestly think that there is no KGB presence in Reykjavík right now? These rooms are bugged ... our movements tracked ... our dealings with the Americans recorded ... because of course they are!

EFIM: You think this could be us?

NIKOLAI: We cannot be certain of anything. We have more immediate concerns.

EFIM: This cannot be allowed.

NIKOLAI: I wish I had your certainty. I wish that *whatever this is* fitted so neatly within my worldview that there was no room left for doubt ... that I could be confident in chucking around words like 'cheat' and 'liar' and 'betrayal' without concern for consequence or fallout.

EFIM: The Americans have acted in a way that is not true to the spirit of the game. They have cheated. The tournament is void. This is incontrovertible proof.

NIKOLAI: We are in the midst of a stand-off involving ICBMs and Doomsday devices ... and you keep adding straw to the camel's back. Enough of this.

BORIS enters.

NIKOLAI: You look like hell. What have you eaten today?

BORIS: Cluck cluck cluck, mother hen.

EFIM: Do you want me to order you some room service?

BORIS: No.

NIKOLAI: He's concerned his food is being tampered with.

EFIM: Are you being serious?

NIKOLAI: Specifically his orange juice. I had a sample sent back to Russia … it came back clean. There were no unusual traces … just juice … just orange juice … a bit of pulp. The Sports Committee is satisfied.

EFIM: He looks fine … you look fine.

BORIS: It was making me lethargic.

EFIM: It's to be expected at this stage of the competition. The opening flurry is well behind us … and there is always a natural plateau. Now it becomes about endurance … fitness … but I would be concerned if he wasn't feeling a little run down.

BORIS: Have we heard back about the X-rays?

NIKOLAI: The FIDE want to scan the chair for a second time before any decision is made.

EFIM: I'm pretty confident that they'll find the proof we …

BORIS: *(Exhausted, to NIKOLAI.)* Are you on top of this?

NIKOLAI: I am.

BORIS: Then I don't need the details.

NIKOLAI: You have to eat something.

BORIS: I need to keep my head clear.

EFIM: I'll order the food, if you're that worried … no one will know that it's meant for you.

BORIS: That's a good idea … had you not just said it out loud for the lamp and the light fittings to hear. *(Beat.)* Sorry. *(Beat.)* Where's Iivo? He should be back by now.

NIKOLAI: You don't have to be here for this.

EFIM: It is better to present a united front.

BORIS: I am sure there is a reasonable explanation.

EFIM: It hardly matters. You should be grateful ... this all deflects attention from you.

BORIS: Me?

NIKOLAI: The American press has been speculating about your possible defection. It's the same template for any high-profile Soviet abroad.

BORIS: It's ridiculous ... and it's certainly not necessary to sacrifice Iivo ... just to distract from some half-hearted lies about my defection. Let them say what they want.

NIKOLAI: It's true that the Americans like their tall tales. But their speculation ... their *theorising* ... it all has repercussions back home ... for us ... for our families.

BORIS: Those scare stories are stale.

EFIM: Then Iivo has nothing to worry about and we have nothing to protect him from. *(Beat.)* He has brought this on himself.

IIVO enters.

IIVO: What are you all doing in my room?

NIKOLAI: Iivo ...

IIVO: What is this? Have the autopsies come back on those two flies?

NIKOLAI: Take a seat.

EFIM: Where have you been?

IIVO: Just for a walk ... along the front ... along the sea fortifications ... down by the ...

NIKOLAI: We know you've been meeting with the Americans.

A deathly silence falls on the room.

EFIM: Okay … I'm going to lay out what we think … what we believe to be true … how we understand the situation to be … and then you'll have a chance to either refute or deny anything that you deem to be false.

IIVO: I'm not entirely sure what I'm supposed to have done.

EFIM: Then let me tell you. Robert Byrne … the American chess player … Grandmaster …

NIKOLAI: He won the US Championship this year, I believe.

EFIM: Did he? Good for him. He's in Reykjavík currently … I've seen him around … we've all seen him. I don't think he's officially attached to Fischer's team … he's just here of his own volition. And you have been meeting with him … between games …

IIVO: I can see how things must look …

BORIS: Don't wriggle … don't squirm … own it and we can move on.

IIVO: Boris, I … this can all be easily explained.

BORIS: So explain it.

IIVO: *(Nothing.)*

BORIS: We all know each other … the chess playing fraternity … we all play each other … and friendships can form over chessboards despite barriers of language or politics … so two friends meeting … having a conversation … sharing a cigarette or a cup of coffee … like opposing border guards at Checkpoint Charlie … that can be overlooked …

IIVO: Boris … I have never … and I would never … betray you …

BORIS: Please. Don't insult me.

EFIM: One coffee ... one dinner ... maybe dinner and a film ... but between every single game ...?

Silence.

IIVO: We're writing a book.

Silence.

EFIM: What?

NIKOLAI: You're writing a book?

IIVO: Yes.

EFIM: A chess book?

IIVO: It's not a ... a ... detective novel! He approached me ... he said he had an idea for a book. There are millions of people across the globe itching for an insight into Spassky ... into Fischer ... so why not write a book? We only ever discuss the games just gone ... never the next game ... never the tactics for the following game. I would want to read such a book ... people all over the world would want to read it ... someone's going to write it ... so why not me?

BORIS: You should have told us.

IIVO: But you'd have made me stop! Wouldn't you?

NIKOLAI: Yes.

BORIS: I fought for you ... for your place on this team ... against advice ... against the wishes of our superiors ...

IIVO: I haven't sold you out.

EFIM: It's not a question of personal loyalty ... if you're passing secrets to the Americans ...

IIVO: It's not like we're discussing atomic research ... it's not like I'm funnelling state secrets ...

EFIM: So you say.

IIVO: I ... I'm *not* ... does it need to be said?

NIKOLAI: This is a lot more serious than I think you realise.

EFIM: If *we* can find out about it ... if the three of us are troubled ... how do you think it'll look to the Kremlin?

NIKOLAI: Are you going to defect?

IIVO: I wasn't thinking of ... I wasn't thinking ...

BORIS: No, you weren't.

NIKOLAI: We get to travel the world ... we get to smoke Western brand cigarettes ... go to the cinema ... see places and ways of living our fellow countrymen do not ... we get to dip our toe in the West ... and it can be very beguiling ... we are high risk and high value ... do you understand that?

IIVO: I am not being groomed by the West and I don't want to defect. I don't want to defect. I am loyal. *(Beat.)* Boris?

BORIS: *(No response.)*

IIVO: What happens now?

NIKOLAI: We've informed the Sports Committee of your decision to fly home. They'll be expecting you on a flight this evening.

EFIM: The ticket's been booked and your suitcase has been packed.

BORIS: Thank you, Iivo. Goodbye.

GAME SEVENTEEN

SPASSKY (WHITE) vs FISCHER (BLACK)

PIRC DEFENSE

DRAW

1.e4 d6 2.d4 g6 3.Nc3 Nf6 4.f4 Bg7 5.Nf3 c5 6.dxc5 Qa5
7.Bd3 Qxc5 8.Qe2 0-0 9.Be3 Qa5 10.0-0 Bg4 11.Rad1 Nc6
12.Bc4 Nh5 13.Bb3 Bxc3 14.bxc3 Qxc3 15.f5 Nf6 16.h3
Bxf3 17.Qxf3 Na5 18.Rd3 Qc7 19.Bh6 Nxb3 20.cxb3
Qc5+ 21.Kh1 Qe5 22.Bxf8 Rxf8 23.Re3 Rc8 24.fxg6
hxg6 25.Qf4 Qxf4 26.Rxf4 Nd7 27.Rf2 Ne5 28.Kh2
Rc1 29.Ree2 Nc6 30.Rc2 Re1 31.Rfe2 Ra1 32.Kg3 Kg7
33.Rcd2 Rf1 34.Rf2 Re1 35.Rfe2 Rf1 36.Re3 a6 37.Rc3
Re1 38.Rc4 Rf1 39.Rdc2 Ra1 40.Rf2 Re1 41.Rfc2 g5
42.Rc1 Re2 43.R1c2 Re1 44.Rc1 Re2 45.R1c2

BORIS SPASSKY (USSR)

7

ROBERT FISCHER (USA)

10

GAME EIGHTEEN

FISCHER (WHITE) vs SPASSKY (BLACK)

SICILIAN RAUZER

DRAW

1.e4 c5 2.Nf3 d6 3.Nc3 Nc6 4.d4 cxd4 5.Nxd4 Nf6 6.Bg5
e6 7.Qd2 a6 8.0-0-0 Bd7 9.f4 Be7 10.Nf3 b5 11.Bxf6 gxf6
12.Bd3 Qa5 13.Kb1 b4 14.Ne2 Qc5 15.f5 a5 16.Nf4 a4
17.Rc1 Rb8 18.c3 b3 19.a3 Ne5 20.Rhf1 Nc4 21.Bxc4
Qxc4 22.Rce1 Kd8 23.Ka1 Rb5 24.Nd4 Ra5 25.Nd3 Kc7

26.Nb4 h5 27.g3 Re5 28.Nd3 Rb8 29.Qe2 Ra5 30.fxe6
fxe6 31.Rf2 e5 32.Nf5 Bxf5 33.Rxf5 d5 34.exd5 Qxd5
35.Nb4 Qd7 36.Rxh5 Bxb4 37.cxb4 Rd5 38.Rc1+ Kb7
39.Qe4 Rc8 40.Rb1 Kb6 41.Rh7 Rd4 42.Qg6 Qc6 43.Rf7
Rd6 44.Qh6 Qf3 45.Qh7 Qc6 46.Qh6 Qf3 47.Qh7 Qc6

BORIS SPASSKY (USSR)

7.5

ROBERT FISCHER (USA)

10.5

GAME NINETEEN

SPASSKY (WHITE) vs FISCHER (BLACK)

ALEKHINE'S DEFENCE

DRAW

1.e4 Nf6 2.e5 Nd5 3.d4 d6 4.Nf3 Bg4 5.Be2 e6 6.0-0 Be7
7.h3 Bh5 8.c4 Nb6 9.Nc3 0-0 10.Be3 d5 11.c5 Bxf3 12.Bxf3
Nc4 13.b3 Nxe3 14.fxe3 b6 15.e4 c6 16.b4 bxc5 17.bxc5
Qa5 18.Nxd5 Bg5 19.Bh5 cxd5 20.Bxf7+ Rxf7 21.Rxf7
Qd2 22.Qxd2 Bxd2 23.Raf1 Nc6 24.exd5 exd5 25.Rd7
Be3+ 26.Kh1 Bxd4 27.e6 Be5 28.Rxd5 Re8 29.Re1 Rxe6
30.Rd6 Kf7 31.Rxc6 Rxc6 32.Rxe5 Kf6 33.Rd5 Ke6
34.Rh5 h6 35.Kh2 Ra6 36.c6 Rxc6 37.Ra5 a6 38.Kg3 Kf6
39.Kf3 Rc3+ 40.Kf2 Rc2+

BORIS SPASSKY (USSR)

8

ROBERT FISCHER (USA)

11

GAME TWENTY

FISCHER (WHITE) vs SPASSKY (BLACK)

SICILIAN RAUZER

DRAW

1.e4 c5 2.Nf3 Nc6 3.d4 cxd4 4.Nxd4 Nf6 5.Nc3 d6 6.Bg5
e6 7.Qd2 a6 8.0-0-0 Bd7 9.f4 Be7 10.Be2 0-0 11.Bf3 h6
12.Bh4 Nxe4 13.Bxe7 Nxd2 14.Bxd8 Nxf3 15.Nxf3 Rfxd8
16.Rxd6 Kf8 17.Rhd1 Ke7 18.Na4 Be8 19.Rxd8 Rxd8
20.Nc5 Rb8 21.Rd3 a5 22.Rb3 b5 23.a3 a4 24.Rc3 Rd8
25.Nd3 f6 26.Rc5 Rb8 27.Rc3 g5 28.g3 Kd6 29.Nc5 g4
30.Ne4+ Ke7 31.Ne1 Rd8 32.Nd3 Rd4 33.Nef2 h5 34.Rc5
Rd5 35.Rc3 Nd4 36.Rc7+ Rd7 37.Rxd7+ Bxd7 38.Ne1
e5 39.fxe5 fxe5 40.Kd2 Bf5 41.Nd1 Kd6 42.Ne3 Be6
43.Kd3 Bf7 44.Kc3 Kc6 45.Kd3 Kc5 46.Ke4 Kd6 47.Kd3
Bg6+ 48.Kc3 Kc5 49.Nd3+ Kd6 50.Ne1 Kc6 51.Kd2 Kc5
52.Nd3+ Kd6 53.Ne1 Ne6 54.Kc3 Nd4

BORIS SPASSKY (USSR)

8.5

ROBERT FISCHER (USA)

11.5

Laugardalshöll arena.

GUÐMUNDUR, under the supervision of LOTHAR, is dismantling the chairs.

MAX is inspecting two sets of X-rays.

NIKOLAI and EFIM stand to one side.

GUÐMUNDUR: There is nothing here.

EFIM: What does that mean?

GUÐMUNDUR: It means ... that there is nothing here.

MAX: The first X-ray clearly shows a *something* ... that a *something* was present.

LOTHAR: But the second X-ray does not.

GUÐMUNDUR: Whatever it is ... or was ... is not here now.

EFIM: What *is* there?

GUÐMUNDUR: Nothing. An emptiness.

EFIM: That proves ...

LOTHAR: What does it prove?

EFIM: ... that whatever was there has been removed ... some device ... a micro-computer ... a radio-transmitter ...

MAX: No one is arguing against that. But without anything in our hands ...

EFIM: The Americans have cheated.

MAX: *(To NIKOLAI.)* Do you agree?

NIKOLAI: Efim's opinions do not reflect the official position of the Russian team.

LOTHAR: Is there anything to suggest what might have been present?

GUÐMUNDUR: No. Nothing.

LOTHAR: Then what else can we do?

EFIM: Void it! Void it all! This entire tournament ... Fischer's mind games ... his lateness ... his idiot demands ... the fuss over the lighting and the cameras ... arbitrary delays ... talk of chemical substances ... suspicions of spiked food and drink ... and no one can rule out mesmerism ... psychic attack. I have known Boris for many years and I have never seen him so struck ... so depleted ... during a match. We demand that the arena be closed off ...

NIKOLAI: Stop.

EFIM: ... and a thorough investigation launched into ...

NIKOLAI: Efim ... stop.

EFIM: You are not the only one who can speak to Moscow.

LOTHAR: The arena has been swept repeatedly ... for bugs ... for devices. We have had Soviets in here with Geiger Counters ... Americans with decibel meters ... we have X-rayed the chair multiple times ... hospital resources are being used and ... and honestly ... it is probably for the best that we have not found anything suspicious.

EFIM: Those X-rays are suspicious.

LOTHAR: A mistake ... an error ... a screwdriver left behind during manufacture ... who's to say?

MAX: It doesn't matter. And I would as soon believe that you Soviets had planted something just to cast suspicion on your opponents.

LOTHAR: There have been so many accusations that the idea of truth has lost all shape and meaning. But we have to believe that the chess … that the *game* … remains one of perfect information. If we were to discover after it all that we have given over our lives to what turns out to be an *imperfect* one … then … then what even is the world? *(Beat.)* What a fucking mess.

MAX: Nikolai … if there's nothing else?

NIKOLAI: *(Shakes his head.)*

MAX: Very well. *(Beat.)* What I've always loved about chess is that a child can learn it in ten minutes. It really is a very simple game. And yet all of this … all of this circus has grown around it … the expenditure of time and effort … of geniuses … of nation states … the literature … and now television has found us … and *money*. But it is still … at its heart … simple. The old can play with the young … the able-bodied with the not … you don't even need common language … it's like music in that sense … intensely human. But I never thought it could be used as a weapon of war … maybe only a propaganda war … but it's a fool who doesn't fear well-deployed propaganda. *(Beat.)* Gentlemen.

MAX, LOTHAR and GUÐMUNDUR exit.

EFIM: Do the X-rays count for nothing?

NIKOLAI: Enough.

EFIM: Something was in his chair.

NIKOLAI: Yes. And then something wasn't. And that's all we know.

EFIM: It cannot stand!

NIKOLAI: Why not?

EFIM: It is not the way that things should be done.

NIKOLAI: Oh my God ... an international sporting tournament is being used to further the agendas of nation states! I'm *shocked!* You should probably get on the phone to the Olympic Committee. I have FIFA's number round here somewhere.

EFIM: So we do nothing?

NIKOLAI: We are the cover under which our nation's security services work ... we are the public face ... the veneer. We should do what is expected of us ... and nothing more. *(Beat.)* I'll inform the Sports Committee. Pass it back up the chain. It is enough.

EFIM: It was not a Soviet device.

NIKOLAI: All the spaces ... all the doubts ... all the uncertainties we encounter in our lives ... we fill them with what we want to be true. So go ahead. Believe what you need to believe.

EFIM: I believe that ... stripped of undue outside influence ... that Boris can still win this tournament.

NIKOLAI: We are due to play game twenty-one in a best of twenty-four championship. There is maybe one game – maybe two – before the gravity of Fischer's advantage pulls it to a close. Do you seriously believe that Boris can win three times on the trot from his current position?

Silence.

EFIM: We have a game to prepare for.

8

The Loftleiðir Hotel – BOBBY's hotel room.

BOBBY and his mother, REGINA FISCHER.

REGINA is in disguise – a horrendous blonde wig and sunglasses.

BOBBY: What's wrong with your hair?

REGINA: It's a wig.

BOBBY: Why are you wearing a wig?

REGINA: I didn't want to be recognised.

BOBBY: Who would recognise you?

REGINA: This hotel is crawling with journalists.

BOBBY: I don't see why they would be interested in you.

REGINA: I didn't want to cause you any trouble.

BOBBY: You don't look like you.

REGINA: Shall I take it off?

BOBBY: Yes.

REGINA: *(Removes her wig and sunglasses.)* Hello, Bobby.

BOBBY: Hello, Mother.

REGINA: So.

BOBBY: Do you want money?

REGINA: No, I don't want money.

BOBBY: Reflected glory?

REGINA: No.

BOBBY: Then what?

REGINA: To see your face.

BOBBY: Turn on a television. *(Beat.)* I don't understand why you are here.

REGINA: I don't want to distract you from the tournament …

BOBBY: You won't.

REGINA: … but this … this is everything we've ever worked for. It felt wrong not to be near you … not to share this moment with you.

BOBBY: Two hundred and fifty thousand dollars.

REGINA: Excuse me?

BOBBY: Two hundred and fifty thousand dollars.

REGINA: Is that how much …?

BOBBY: It's how much I'm getting.

REGINA: For playing?

BOBBY: For winning.

REGINA: Well.

BOBBY: You were wrong. Chess makes money.

REGINA: I only wanted what was best for you.

BOBBY: What was best for me was that I played chess. So you were wrong.

REGINA: They said you were sick … that you were delayed in New York because you were ill.

BOBBY: I am the fittest I have ever been.

REGINA: Sickness doesn't have to be in the body.

BOBBY: You think I'm a nutbar.

REGINA: No.

BOBBY: You think I'm a Froot Loop.

REGINA: I have struggled ... I can see you struggle ...

BOBBY: I am not you.

REGINA: No.

BOBBY: They'll take your money ... that's all they want ... when you should spend it on food ... on clothes ... they'll take your money and tell you you're sick ... make up brain diseases ... invent disorders ... they call you crazy so they can take your money. Psychiatry ... it's a racket ... and we all know who runs it. Filling your head ... telling you to be one way ... telling you it's better than the way you are ... well the way I am is that I am the world champion! Top player. Top of the heap. So what do they know ... what do they know?

REGINA: No one ever tried to put an idea in your head.

BOBBY: Psychiatrists should be paying me ... working on my brain would be a privilege ... best of all time ... best of all time ...

Silence.

REGINA: You're ahead. That's good.

BOBBY: It is.

REGINA: Near the end.

BOBBY: Yes.

REGINA: Would it distract you were I to be in the audience?

BOBBY: Yes.

REGINA: Let me see your teeth.

BOBBY: No.

REGINA: Your breath stinks. Let me see your teeth.

BOBBY: *(Opens his mouth for her.)*

REGINA: Where are your fillings?

BOBBY: I don't have any.

REGINA: You had a number of fillings.

BOBBY: I had them removed.

REGINA: Why, Bobby?

BOBBY: I don't want people putting things in my head.

REGINA: Your teeth will fall out ... they'll rot.

BOBBY: It doesn't matter.

REGINA: I want you to do well. Haven't I always wanted you to do well?

BOBBY: Best of all time.

REGINA: So you say.

BOBBY: Best. Of. All. Time. *(Beat.)* I am not a child.

REGINA: No.

BOBBY: I do not want you here.

REGINA: You have made that clear. You have always made that clear. And haven't I always done as you've asked? When you were sixteen ... I moved out ... I left the apartment to yourself and your sister ... at your request. I gave you what you wanted ... such a special talent ... haven't I given you everything you ever wanted? I have not seen you for ten years ... I have stayed away for ten years ... because that is what you asked of me. Are you

not happy? You could have been anything ... why have
you chosen to be this?

BOBBY: I am the best.

REGINA: Let me enjoy this moment. Let me see my son
achieve what he always wanted to achieve. Let me see my
son happy.

BOBBY: I don't know what that's supposed to look like ...
I've never seen it before ... I've never known it ... How
am I supposed to put it together from broken bits? *(Beat.)*
There are Communists in this hotel.

REGINA: I am sure there are.

BOBBY: Go and knock on their door. They may want you.
There are Jews there too. You will feel right at home.

REGINA: *(Doesn't leave.)*

BOBBY: They tried to tell me that chess wasn't chess. They
tried to tell me about Freud ... about Oedipus ... that
taking the king was killing the father ... a father-murder-
fantasy game. The queen ... the powerful ... the mother.
I tried to tell them the king wasn't a king ... it was just
a piece of often-wood that could move one square in
any direction. The bishop used to be an elephant ... a
messenger ... a jester ... a madman. And a castle can't
move. I can play both black and white. I can hold in my
mind both halves of the game at once ... and keep them
separate ... so that my black-self doesn't know what my
white-self is planning. You can only truly know someone
when you destroy them ... like a cannibal takes the
strength of his opponent in the eating ... and that is what
I do when I am at the chessboard ... but increasingly
everything is so bland ... because I am at the top now ...
so who is there left to destroy?

REGINA: *(Comforts him, kissing him gently on the forehead.)*

BOBBY: Get your hands off me – they're dirty. You're dirty. A filthy dirty pig. Jew.

REGINA: *(Steps away.)* I am glad you are doing well, Bobby. I wish only the best for you. I hope you get what you need.

BOBBY: What I *need* is what is due me. What I need is for the universe to be a single star. What I need is for everyone to blink out of existence when I exit a room. I want no before and no after. I want to ascend above the stink and sweat … the body odour and athlete's foot … the pimples and boils of other people. I want my mind in space … a clear white space … beyond this cheap, physical world with its history and people … its politics and compromise … its lies and deceptions. I want to tear down this world … burn down this world … so that all that remains is Bobby Fischer. That is what it means to win. I want to win.

GAME TWENTY-ONE

SPASSKY (WHITE) vs FISCHER (BLACK)

SICILIAN TAIMANOV

WHITE RESIGNS

1.e4 c5 2.Nf3 e6 3.d4 cxd4 4.Nxd4 a6 5.Nc3 Nc6 6.Be3 Nf6 7.Bd3 d5 8.exd5 exd5 9.0-0 Bd6 10.Nxc6 bxc6 11.Bd4 0-0 12.Qf3 Be6 13.Rfe1 c5 14.Bxf6 Qxf6 15.Qxf6 gxf6 16.Rad1 Rfd8 17.Be2 Rab8 18.b3 c4 19.Nxd5 Bxd5 20.Rxd5 Bxh2+ 21.Kxh2 Rxd5 22.Bxc4 Rd2 23.Bxa6 Rxc2 24.Re2 Rxe2 25.Bxe2 Rd8 26.a4 Rd2 27.Bc4 Ra2 28.Kg3 Kf8 29.Kf3 Ke7 30.g4 f5 31.gxf5 f6 32.Bg8 h6 33.Kg3 Kd6 34.Kf3 Ra1 35.Kg2 Ke5 36.Be6 Kf4 37.Bd7 Rb1 38.Be6 Rb2 39.Bc4 Ra2 40.Be6 h5 41.Bd7

BORIS SPASSKY (USSR)

8.5

ROBERT FISCHER (USA)

12.5

BOBBY wins. He is triumphant.

9.

Bessastaðir – the President of Iceland's official residence.

A grand end of tournament party – black tie, loud music, dancing.

A laurel wreath is placed around BOBBY's neck. A cheque giving ceremony. Champagne and standing ovations. Music. Dancing.

BOBBY is closely examining his winner's cheque.

BORIS approaches.

BORIS: I just wanted to take the opportunity to congratulate you.

BOBBY: *(Points to the name on the cheque.)* Robert James Fischer.

BORIS: It was my honour to play against you.

BOBBY: Your team spread rumours … that I poisoned your orange juice … that I hypnotised you … that I had teams of lackeys and minions feeding chess moves to me via ear-piece. I didn't hypnotise you. I didn't do any of that. If anyone cheated, you cheated. And what did it get you? Nothing. A whole bag of nothing. A whole suitcase. *(Points again to the cheque.)* Robert James Fischer.

BORIS: If my side interfered with the game, I was unaware of it. If there was any kind of interference, it was obviously ineffective. *(Beat.)* Don't leave that behind … your wreath

... bay leaves. My wife still cooks with the leaves from mine. *(Beat.)* I suppose I should say something grand ... something to mark the occasion. I was at the table ... you were at the table ... there is what I know and there is what you know ... somewhere amongst all of that is the truth.

BOBBY: Cheating is not winning.

BORIS: It is also not losing.

BOBBY: No. *(Beat.)* There were some good games.

BORIS: There were. I hope to play you again someday.

BOBBY: If the money is right. *(Beat.)* How old are you?

BORIS: What ...?

BOBBY: How old are you?

BORIS: I'm thirty-five.

BOBBY: There's six years between us.

BORIS: Is that important?

BOBBY: I am your better.

BORIS: So says the base of the trophy.

BOBBY: I am not a child.

BORIS: I never said you were. *(Beat.)* You want to say we met as equals? Yes, we met as equals. You want to say you outplayed me? Yes, you outplayed me. You want to say you are my better? I am not going to stop you. I am proud to have played you, Bobby Fischer. I am proud to have played those beautiful games. But I am also tired. It is a lot to carry. I daresay your American burdens will be somewhat different to the expectations I've shouldered ... but there is some relief for me in all of this. Let me give you some advice ... from one world champion to another.

It will be hard for you. You will feel like a god. You will feel unstoppable. When you want something for so long … when you define yourself by the wanting of it … it can be disarming to finally … to finally achieve … do you understand? You think it will solve all your problems … but often it only magnifies them. It will bring you friends who are not your friends … lovers without love … and you will have no control over how other people see you … how the world sees you. And that will infuriate you like nothing else before. *(Beat.)* I must drink more champagne.

BOBBY: I beat you.

BORIS: You did.

BOBBY: I won.

BORIS: Well done.

BOBBY: Best of all time.

10.

The Loftleiðir Hotel – foyer.

NIKOLAI and EFIM wait with their suitcases – they look tired, beaten.

NIKOLAI: I'm going to get some air.

EFIM: It's raining.

NIKOLAI: Then I'll take an umbrella.

EFIM: It's that sort of preparation and forethought that has so far been lacking on this trip.

NIKOLAI: Is that our defence then? Our strategy? Is that we will tell them? That Boris was underprepared?

EFIM: He thought he could play honestly. His views on
    bourgeois sportsmanship scuppered us. His trust in the
    sport was naïve.

BORIS enters with a suitcase.

NIKOLAI: Our car should be here in …

BORIS: Just put me on the plane. The details don't matter.

NIKOLAI: There are going to be questions asked …

BORIS: Then let them be asked back home. We have a three-
    hour flight to Copenhagen … and from Copenhagen then
    on to Moscow … let me have my time … these last few
    moments outside the state machinery.

NIKOLAI: I think our taxi has arrived.

NIKOLAI and EFIM go to leave, but BORIS stays where he is.

BORIS: I haven't walked those streets … entered those rooms
    … those Russian rooms … those Soviet rooms … the
    Moscow Central Chess Club … having lost a title before.
    I can't see the next move. I don't know what it looks like.
    I first learnt this damn game when I was four years old …
    born in Leningrad … a child of war. We were evacuated
    … taken to an orphanage … myself and my older brother.
    There was a chessboard and some of the children knew
    the rules. We would sometimes hear news from home …
    things people had seen … done … rumours and trauma.
    We had friends there still … family … neighbours.
    Unburied bodies in the streets … limbs … rubble
    … hunger. People did desperate things to survive …
    animalistic things. I am sure you saw war but you did not
    see Leningrad. How can a child process *chaos* on such a
    scale? Chess was an escape … a simple universe … simple
    in its movements … yet still it contains infinities. And I
    stayed there for a while … we all did … hiding in that

world of kings, knights and rooks. I stayed there for a long time. Stayed there through Stalin ... through Khruschev ... through Brezhnev. But it seems that chaos has found me again ... and I ... and I ... *(Beat.)* I should be cursing his name. I should hate him. In a long match such as this ... a player can travel very deep inside himself ... into dark unlit depths ... and when it's all done ... you come to the surface very fast. Every time after a tournament ... if I win or lose ... I become so incredibly depressed. People seem alien to me ... friends seem like strangers ... because no one knows me like he does ... no one has struggled with me ... wrestled with me ... on such a fundamental level. It's ridiculous but I miss him already.

END.

Russian Translation

Translation by Oksana Dovorecka.

The English line is followed by its Russian (Cyrillic) translation and finally a transliterated line to assist with pronunciation. Bold text indicates emphasis.

1.1

EFIM:	Stop.
	Прекрати
	Pre-Cra-**tea**

IIVO:	What?
	чего?
	tschee-**vo**

EFIM	Stop shaking your leg.
	Ногой дергать прекрати
	noh-**goy der**-gatt Pre-cra-**tee**

IIVO	I'm not shaking my …
	Ничего я не дергаю …
	Nee-che-**go** ya ne **der**-gah-yoo

EFIM	You are.
	Дергаешь
	Der-gah-esh

IIVO	I can shake my leg if I want.
	Хочу и дергаю
	Kha-**choo** ee **der**-ga-yoo

EFIM	Why does a man shake his leg, Nikolai? Is it symptomatic of something?
	Николай, а с чего человек ногой дергает? Это симптом какой?
	Nee-koh-**lai** ah s tschee-**vo** che-love-**ehk** noh-**goy** **der**-gah-et? Eh-to sim-**ptom** kah-**koi**

NIKOLAI	A soothing ritual. Don't read too much into it.
	Успокаивается он так. Не обращай внимания.
	oos-pah-**kah**-eevaetsya on tak. Nye ob-rah-**schay** vnee-**mah**-nee-ya

1.3

EFIM	I knew it.
	я знал
	Ya znal

1.8

BORIS	This is insane.
	Это безумие
	Eh-to Bez-**ooh**-mie

9 781786 829320